THE
ESSENTIAL
WOK
COOKBOOK

THE ESSENTIAL WOK COOKBOOK

A Simple Chinese Cookbook
for Stir-Fry, Dim Sum,
and Other Restaurant Favorites

Naomi Imatome-Yun

ROCKRIDGE
PRESS

Interior photographs © Gabriel (Gabi) Bucataru/Stocksy, pg. 2; Andrew Scrivani/Stockfood, pg. 5; Valerie Janssen/Stockfood, pg. 6; Sheri Giblin/Stockfood, pg. 10; Mick Shippen/ Stockfood, pg. 23; Dana Hoff/Stockfood, pg. 28; Jean Cazals/Stockfood, pg. 50; Jean Cazals/ Stockfood, pg. 66; Nadine Greeff/Stocksy, pg. 78; Klaus Arras/Stockfood, pg. 94; Gräfe & Unzer Verlag/Jörn Rynio/Stockfood, pg. 112; Nadine Greeff/Stocksy, pg. 130. All other photographs Shutterstock and Istock.

ISBN: Print 978-1-62315-605-3 | eBook: 978-1-62315-606-0

CONTENTS

INTRODUCTION

Chinese food has become as American as pizza, bagels, and tacos. It's a comfort food that we enjoy and love, whether we live in big cities or small towns. Although foodies might scoff at Chinese take-out for its lack of authenticity, Chinese food in America is an incredible story of immigration, invention, and adaptation. According to Andrew Coe's *Chop Suey: A Cultural History of Chinese Food in the United States*, there are more than 40,000 Chinese restaurants in the United States, more than all the McDonald's, Burger King, and Wendy's fast-food restaurants put together. But unlike with other beloved regional eats, such as Italian or Mexican fare, many people still don't regularly make Chinese food at home.

This book will teach you that preparing your favorite Chinese restaurant dishes in your own kitchen is simple, healthy, and cost-efficient. You don't even need to go to a special Asian grocery for the bulk of the ingredients, as most supermarket chains now carry the essentials needed to make Chinese food at home. And now that online sites such as Amazon carry hard-to-find spices and seasonings, everything you need is within reach.

There are undeniable conveniences to Chinese delivery: It is fast (usually ready in 30 to 45 minutes), easy (a quick phone call or online order), and satisfying. But, like most fast food, it's not always the healthiest option.

Chinese home cooking is a lot less salty, oily, and heavy than its restaurant take-out counterparts. It's also packed with fresh ingredients. Although those ubiquitous white boxes have their charm, you will be surprised to learn how simple it is to make healthy Chinese dishes at home. And you'll save money while you're at it.

The secret to cooking delicious Chinese food at home is the wok: a large pan with a bowl-like shape that has either two handles or one long wooden handle. With just this one pan, you can make thousands of tasty dishes quickly and cheaply. Yes, *thousands*. Many American homes have a wok or a woklike pan in their collection of kitchen equipment; it's a favorite for preparing stir-fries of all kinds. And although it *is* the perfect pan to use for great-tasting stir-fries, the wok has so much more potential. There's a reason that the Chinese have used the wok for more than two thousand years with very few changes to the pan itself. In addition to stir-frying, you can also steam, boil, stew, braise, deep-fry, poach, smoke, sear, and sauté in a wok. The recipes in this book were designed to highlight the versatility of this time-tested piece of kitchen equipment—the wok is the only pan you will need to cook your way through these pages.

The recipes in this cookbook are designed with the take-out lover in mind. Unnecessary salt, unneeded oil, and undesirable ingredients, such as MSG, have been eliminated without sacrificing flavor. You won't miss anything by cooking this way. You may even come to prefer it.

Think about flavor-packed Kung Pao Chicken, crispy egg rolls, and comforting wonton soup. Consider spicy eggplant with garlic and mu shu vegetables. They all hit a different spot, and now you can enjoy healthier versions of your favorite Chinese dishes at home. So let's fire up the wok and start cooking!

1

EVERYDAY CHINESE COOKING

If you grew up eating Chinese food in America, then you might be surprised to learn you likely wouldn't find most of your favorite dishes on a visit to China. Much like American cuisine, Chinese cuisine itself is not one thing, as China is a huge country and its different regions have very different ways of preparing food, based on local ingredients. Chinese food in America is the product of immigration, local tastes, and American ingredients, which have influenced the evolution of the cuisine since the Gold Rush days of the 1850s.

During the 1860s, Chinese workers came to California to work on the railroads. Most were working men who came to do hard labor, and they were almost all from rural villages outside Canton (now called Guangzhou). Some of these new immigrants opened Chinese restaurants, hoping to provide the familiar flavors of home. So Chinese food in America got its start very loosely from Cantonese cooking. The immigrants were not trained chefs, and they didn't have the same vegetables, herbs, or spices they were used to in China. Instead, they had to improvise, using non-Chinese ingredients, such as broccoli, yellow onion, pineapple, and carrot, in their food.

It was during the next hundred or so years that the Chinese American dishes of chow mein, wonton soup, chop suey, moo goo gai pan, and egg foo young were created and introduced around America. In this time, Chinese immigrants traveled to different parts of America, often establishing Chinatowns, where large groups of immigrants settled. With them, they brought their knowledge of their cuisine and adapted it to include what was available.

The US government severely curtailed Chinese immigration in the late 1800s. It wasn't until 1965 that American immigration laws for Chinese people changed, and the doors opened to a new wave of immigrants from Hong Kong and Taiwan. These new immigrants landed mostly in cities, and it is this second wave that gave birth to the American standards of Kung Pao Chicken, General Tso's Chicken, and hot and sour soup.

Today, Chinese noodles, egg rolls, and sweet and sour pork are as beloved by Americans as pizza and hot dogs. Ordering Chinese food for delivery or take-out and enjoying a meal that arrives in overstuffed white containers is a familiar part of American culture.

WOK BASICS

The wok is an integral part of Chinese cooking because its unique shape and surface area make it good not just for stir-frying, but also for braising, stewing, poaching, steaming, deep-frying, and even smoking. The traditional wok, used for almost 2,000 years, has a rounded bottom, which easily allows a spatula or other utensil to move the food around the pan.

Wok hay, or *wok hei*, is a Cantonese phrase used to describe a well-made stir-fry dish. It translates as "breath of a wok," and it refers to the concentrated, rich flavor that can come only from making a stir-fry in a well-seasoned wok over very high heat.

CHOOSING A WOK

There are so many different types of woks on the market that it can be dizzying to choose the right one for your needs. When buying a wok, don't be fooled into thinking that the most expensive one is the best choice. A $10 carbon steel wok purchased in Chinatown can be perfect for home cooking needs.

➤ 12- or 14-inch Flat-Bottomed Carbon Steel Wok

This pan is really your best choice. Light and easy to handle, a carbon steel wok develops a nonstick surface after you season it, so you don't have to use much oil when cooking. It also heats up quickly, conducts heat well, and cools down quickly, which is essential for good stir-fry technique.

Most home stoves cannot get as hot as professional stoves or traditional Chinese stoves (on which the wok sits in the flames). The flat-bottomed wok makes up for this lack because it covers more of the heat than its round-bottomed cousin. If you don't cook large meals and are cooking for one or two, then a 12-inch wok will be good for you. For families, a 14-inch wok will be perfect.

➤ Round-Bottomed Carbon Steel Wok

This traditional Cantonese wok has a round bottom and two handles. Because the rounded-bottom wok isn't stable on the stove, you need to use a wok ring underneath it so it doesn't tip over. For this safety reason, cooks new to a wok may not want to start off with a round-bottomed wok.

➤ Cast Iron Wok

An American cast iron wok is quite heavy and takes longer to heat up, which makes stir-frying a challenge. If that's all you have, don't fret. You can still follow the recipes in this book to make a tasty stir-fry and excellent poached, steamed, braised, and fried dishes. When you get the chance, invest in a lighter, easier-to-use carbon steel wok.

➤ Nonstick Wok or Skillet

Most stir-fry experts don't recommend using this type of wok or skillet because the food won't taste the same. A nonstick wok or skillet cannot reach the high heat level conducted by a carbon steel or cast iron wok, which is necessary to create the best-tasting stir-fries. But if that's what you have at home, you absolutely can go ahead and make these recipes with your nonstick pan. They will still taste great! Once you're ready, get a carbon steel wok and be impressed with the flavor difference.

➤ Electric Wok

This isn't ideal for stir-frying because it doesn't retain heat well, making it difficult to achieve *wok hay*. However, you can use an electric wok happily for poaching, steaming, braising, and stewing.

SEASONING YOUR WOK

When you buy a new carbon steel or cast iron wok, you need to season it before you start cooking with it. Do not season a nonstick wok or an electric wok. Seasoning will take at least 30 minutes, but once done, you'll have created a naturally nonstick surface without the chemicals found in a Teflon coating.

As always when dealing with high heat and oil, be careful and focused during the seasoning process so that you don't burn yourself.

How to Season Your Wok: A Step-by-Step Guide

1. Your carbon steel or cast iron wok will come home from the store smelling like oil. This oil is a preservative applied by the manufacturer. It will need to be cleaned off the wok. Wash the wok in soapy water, and scrub it clean on the inside and the outside.

2. Now you need to "burn" the wok. Place it on the stove, and dry it over very high heat.

3. Remove the wok from the heat, and put a few tablespoons of peanut oil in the bottom of the wok. Using a dry cloth, spread a thin layer of the oil completely over the inside surface of the wok. Be careful not to burn yourself.

4. This next part will get smoky, so turn on your oven fan and open your windows. Over very high heat, heat the oil in the wok for a few minutes. Turn off the heat, take the wok off the heat, and let it cool to room temperature.

5. Once the wok is at room temperature, put it on high heat again, making sure the first layer of oil gets "burned" into the wok. Once it is, turn off the heat, take the pan off the stove, and return the pan to room temperature again.

ORIGIN STORIES | *Wonton Soup*

Wontons and other dumplings have been part of Chinese cuisine for a very long time. Roughly translated from Cantonese, *wonton* means "swallowing clouds" because of the way the white dumplings float in soup. But the wonton soup served at most American-style Chinese restaurants is very different from the dumpling soups served in China. Chinese wontons are plump with a very thin wrapper. One of the most famous types has a juicy shrimp and pork filling. American-style wontons have a very small amount of meat—usually pork—and are covered in a thick, doughy wrapper.

The broth of Americanized wonton soup is a premade watery stock, a stark contrast to the traditional long-simmered pork-based broth found in China. Chinese restaurants in America serve wonton soup in small bowls as an accompaniment to or appetizer before the main part of the meal. Soup is a main course in most regional Chinese cuisines, and it can even be a meal by itself. The American-style wonton soup evolved, over time, based on the need of restaurants to make a quick, tasty dish that wasn't expensive (hence less meat and more filler).

6. Once at room temperature, add another thin layer of oil, and spread it over the inside surface of the wok, as you did in step 3. Heat the wok again for a few minutes, and then turn off the heat, take the pan off the heat, and return it to room temperature once more.

7. Repeat steps 5 and 6 a few more times. Wipe off any excess oil that collects in the bottom center of the wok. Once the wok starts to darken and look shiny, it's ready to use.

8. If you can, do a first stir-fry of sliced onions to remove any unwanted smells from the wok.

The more you cook with your wok, the better its seasoning will be and the less oil you'll have to use when cooking with it. Reseason your wok if it becomes necessary.

CARING FOR YOUR WOK

Employ some simple and basic tips to keep your wok in good condition and ready for use. New woks need oil to continue developing their seasoning layer. So don't do a lot of poaching with a newly seasoned wok—do a lot of stir-frying! Wok expert Grace Young (coauthor with Alan Richardson of *The Breath of a Wok*) recommends making a few batches of popcorn in your wok with peanut oil to speed up the seasoning process. And when cooking, always heat the wok until it's hot before adding oil. Remember that television chef Martin Yan often instructed his viewers to add cold oil to a hot wok so that food wouldn't stick.

Never wash your seasoned wok with soap. Rinse it with warm water, and wipe it with a gentle sponge or brush. Don't abrasively scrub your wok, as that will affect the seasoning layer. Don't use steel pads or scouring sponges on the inside, though you can use them on the outside of your wok if it gets very dirty. For a new wok, you might want to dry it over high heat after you rinse it. For a well-seasoned wok, just wipe until dry. Don't let it sit around wet. It could develop rust if that happens. Over time, your wok will become deeper in color and the seasoning layer will develop. Once this happens, you can just wipe out your wok with a paper towel, like you would a nonstick pan.

The more you cook with your wok, the better seasoned it will be. If you don't use your wok often, rub a small amount of peanut oil onto the inside surface of the wok before storing it. If you forget about your wok for a while and it gets rusty or if it gets very burned once you use it again, then do a full reseasoning of it. In *Stir-Frying to the Sky's Edge*, Grace Young recommends giving it "wok facials" from time to time. To do a wok facial, fold three layers of paper towels into a wad, and set the wad aside. Heat the wok over high heat. Once hot, remove it from the heat, and add a couple of teaspoons of peanut or vegetable oil and some kosher salt (use a 2 to 1 ratio of oil and salt). Using the paper towels, gently rub and scrub the oil and salt all over the inside of your wok until it's clean and shiny. Rinse out the wok with warm water, using a textured sponge to remove any lingering salt crystals. Voilà! Your wok is rejuvenated.

ORIGIN STORIES | *Fortune Cookies*

Opening a crunchy yellow cookie and reading the "fortune" inside is the ritual ending to a meal at an American Chinese restaurant. But these vanilla-flavored cookies are a purely American tradition. They aren't made, served, or eaten in China. In fact, unlike some of our favorite Chinese take-out

foods, they might not even have been invented by a Chinese American. It seems that the original fortune cookies were based on confections made at a Shinto shrine near Kyoto, Japan; there is no consensus on who first started making and serving them in America.

Regardless, they became popular in Chinese restaurants in California after World War II, and these early fortune cookies were usually filled with Bible verses and quotes from Confucius, Benjamin Franklin, and other philosophers. From the West Coast, they spread to every other Chinese take-out joint in the States. Now they are an integral part of every American-style Chinese restaurant meal.

BETTER THAN DELIVERY

American-style Chinese food is convenient and often budget-friendly, but it's still part of American fast-food culture. Cheap and fast generally means unhealthy, and American-style Chinese food is no exception. Like most well-loved convenience foods, take-out Chinese food is full of extra salt and (thanks to the sugar and oil used) extra calories. Many of the most popular dishes are deep-fried, heavily breaded, or covered in a sweet and syrupy sauce. The use of the flavor enhancer MSG (monosodium glutamate) is declining, fortunately, but many places do still use it. MSG occurs naturally in some foods, such as tomatoes, potatoes, and other fruits and vegetables, and it is often added to Chinese food, canned vegetables, and processed meats. Some people have adverse reactions to MSG. According to the Mayo Clinic, some consumers of the flavor enhancer have reported that it caused headaches, sweating, heart palpitations, nausea, or weakness. All the more reason to make your favorite Chinese dishes at home and skip the MSG.

A HEALTHY ALTERNATIVE

Authentic Chinese food, on the other hand, is a healthy cuisine. The Organisation for Economic Co-operation and Development reports that the obesity rate is only 2.9 percent in China. Compare this with the US obesity rate of 35 percent.

So what's the difference between American Chinese take-out and authentic Chinese cuisines?

Vegetables take center stage in traditional Chinese cooking, most ingredients are stir-fried (not deep-fried), and sauces aren't filled with sugar. At your local Chinese establishment, your stir-fried noodles (chow mein or lo mein) or dishes such as beef with broccoli are made with a liberal amount of oil. But that's not actually the correct way to cook in a wok. Because of its unique shape and high heat retention, you need very little oil to cook in a seasoned wok. When cooking in a seasoned wok, the finished meat and vegetables are pushed up the sides of the wok, thus draining the food of a lot of oil while cooking with very little effort.

The recipes in this book were created for those who love take-out Chinese food but want to make tastier and healthier versions at home. So although they are not traditional Chinese recipes, they are in the spirit of traditional Chinese cuisines, emphasizing vegetables, big bowls of soup, and the freshest produce, meats, and fish. Adding these recipes and dishes to your everyday routine (and cutting back on take-out) will do wonders for your wallet, your waistline, and your overall health.

Tips for Healthy Chinese Cooking at Home

Use a lot of vegetables. Fresh and in season is best, but you can use flash-frozen vegetables or bagged ones with great results, too. Chinese stir-fries and soups are easy to improvise, so feel free to be creative with the ingredient lists in recipes.

ORIGIN STORIES | *Sweet and Sour Dishes*

These are loosely based on dishes that exist in China, as sweet, vinegary sauces are part of certain regional Chinese cuisines. But there are many differences between the American versions and their Asian counterparts. Sweet and sour dishes in America, whether they are made with chicken, pork, or shrimp, consist of small pieces of protein stir-fried—sometimes after

first being deep-fried—with green peppers, onions, carrots, and canned pineapple. The sweet and sour sauce is a blend of soy sauce, sugar, ketchup, and vinegar.

Yellow (round) onions, carrots, and pineapple are not native to China, but they were widely available to the first Chinese restaurant owners in America. It'd be hard to recognize our take-out now without them. And because of the need for cost-saving and convenience, Chinese cooks started using canned pineapple and maraschino cherries in their sauces and dishes. They, along with sugar and ketchup, are responsible for a lot of the sweetness in many popular American-style Chinese foods, especially the sweet and sour offerings.

Think beyond stir-fry. You can steam, braise, or poach in a wok with no added oil.

A little protein goes a long way. You need a lot less meat (or seafood) when making Chinese food. A pound of chicken, a lot of vegetables, and steamed rice is a bountiful meal for a family of four.

Spice it up. Traditional Chinese food uses fragrant spices for flavor. Add ginger, garlic, and chiles to your dishes for great flavor without unnecessary sugar or salt.

Keep it light. Don't think of Chinese food as needing to be covered in heavy, sweet sauces. The recipes in this cookbook are delicious, and don't require a heavy hand with soy sauce, sugar, or oil.

From soup to . . . soup. Get to know Chinese soups, which can be made in a wok and are healthy, filling, and comforting. If you're watching your weight, include vegetable-filled, fragrant soups in your meal to enjoy satisfying meals with minimal effort.

Size does matter. Most American restaurants serve huge portions, which leads to overeating. You can stuff yourself without noticing if there are piles of food in front of you. Preparing meals at home lets you practice effortless portion control.

Satisfaction for everyone. For families with young kids, Chinese soups, braises, and stir-fries are a good way to introduce children to different vegetables cooked with flavors they already like.

CUT COSTS

The total cost of a homemade meal is much less than that of a restaurant meal, and that includes fast-food places and Chinese take-out. Two people might spend $20 at either a fast-food restaurant or a chain restaurant, but you can make at least two (most probably three) of the recipes in this book for that amount of money. And if you're making a stir-fry, you can cook and be eating in the time that it would take you to order and then pick up your food.

Money-Saving Tips

Stock up on staples in bulk. You know that you'll always use spices, rice, beans, noodles, soup broth, and frozen vegetables, so get those at your warehouse store or your local grocery when they're on sale. You can freeze meat in resealable bags for later use.

Cook with leftovers in mind. Stir-fries, noodles, and fried rice dishes are flexible leftovers, so you can save time and money by always making a little extra.

Throw out less food. Because of the adaptable nature of casual Chinese home cooking, you can transform yesterday's leftovers into new, delicious meals, reducing food waste.

Eat more vegetables. You will automatically eat less meat per person if you're cooking a lot of these recipes, so keep that in mind while shopping.

Check out a Chinese or Asian grocery store. They have great sales and often great prices on the freshest meat and fish (still swimming!) and produce. And they'll have those harder-to-find ingredients.

Don't worry if you're far from an Asian market. Most of the staples in this book are available at your local grocery store, and what your store does not have are widely available online.

Invest in a rice cooker. Make this small investment as you start learning to cook your Chinese favorites at home—it's so convenient to always have rice on hand. Many dishes in this book can be made in 15 minutes or less, including perfectly cooked rice.

2

THE CHINESE KITCHEN

When you walk into a Chinese market for the first time, you'll see amazing things, from hundreds of types of pickles to shoppers selecting their seafood dinner while it's still swimming. Although it'll be fascinating—and maybe a little intimidating at first—you won't need to buy a lot of exotic ingredients to pull off delicious Chinese meals at home. The recipes in this book are for the home cook, so you won't have to struggle with overly complex preparations or dozens of spices and seasonings that you'll use only once or twice. And because you'll stock your pantry with staples you can use again and again, even in non-Chinese dishes, it won't cost a lot to start cooking Chinese at home. In no time, you'll be a whiz at whipping up a healthy, delicious dinner in your wok in 15 minutes.

These days, large chain grocery stores carry Chinese cooking essentials, including soy sauce, garlic, ginger, cornstarch, oyster sauce, hoisin sauce, jasmine rice, sesame oil, and chili sauce. Although these might not be the most traditional versions, they are a good place to start. In big cities around the country, you'll also be able to buy rice noodles and rice vinegar at your local supermarket, and may never even need to make the trek to Chinatown or your closest Asian market.

THE INGREDIENTS

Once you've stocked up, you can make dozens of delicious, better-than-take-out meals at home. To make it even easier, a list of the top 15 essential ingredients follows. These ingredients can all be purchased online if you can't find them at your grocery store or Asian market. And these staple ingredients, although frequently called for in this cookbook, will last you a long time. Refer to the resources section at the end of this book to find more information about recommended brands and buying Chinese ingredients online.

THE BASICS

These are the basic ingredients that you will find popping up in Chinese recipes again and again. When stocking your pantry for Chinese home cooking, start with these essentials, most of which will be available at your local supermarket.

Garlic: Spicy, fragrant, and versatile, garlic is one of the most common spices that you'll be using. Although you can employ garlic powder in a pinch, try to stock your fridge and freezer with fresh garlic. You can mince it or slice it and then freeze it in resealable plastic bags. You can even buy solo garlic, or single-clove garlic, which simplifies cooking.

Ginger: A little goes a long way, so you don't need to buy large pieces of ginger root. It does, however, add essential flavor and a nice, peppery spice to Chinese dishes. Make things even easier by freezing peeled ginger in small chunks and then grating it when you need it.

Chinese chili sauce: This is a must-have. It costs very little, whether you're buying it at a large grocery chain or at a Chinese grocery. Most Chinese chili sauces are also seasoned with garlic, so having some of this on hand makes seasoning that much easier. You can also use it as a dipping sauce or create new dips out of it.

Cornstarch: In Chinese cooking, cornstarch is mixed with a little water and added to sauces and soups in the later stages of cooking to thicken them. It's also used as part of the marinade in the "velveting" process, which is what makes your take-out chicken, pork, and beef pieces super soft and silky.

Fish sauce: Fish sauce is a thin, slightly stinky liquid made from salted anchovies. It's most often associated with Southeast Asian cooking, but other Asian cuisines use it as well. It's an amber-colored seasoning that adds a lot of flavor in just a little splash. It is also known as *nuoc mam* and *nam pla*.

Noodles: There is amazing variety in Chinese noodles, and they vary according to region of origin, shape, width, texture, and ingredients. Walk into any Chinese grocery, and you'll be amazed at the variety of different types of fresh and dried noodles available, from crispy rice noodles to bean threads to egg noodles. Use noodles in stir-fries, soups, and much more. Start with egg noodles—they're the most common and versatile.

Chinese five-spice powder: This fragrant seasoning mixture is usually a blend of anise, cinnamon, cloves, fennel, and Sichuan (Szechuan) peppercorns. But not all Chinese five-spice powders are the same, so it could also include ginger and black pepper. It's a great seasoning for stir-fries, marinades, and fatty meat dishes.

Hoisin sauce: A thick, rich sauce made from soybean paste, garlic, sugar, and spices, hoisin adds a sweet and savory flavor to stir-fries, marinades, and dipping sauces.

Rice (jasmine, long- or medium-grain): Almost all Chinese dishes are enjoyed with rice, unless you are eating a bowl of noodles or some dumplings. Chinese restaurants in America seem to serve mostly jasmine rice, which is a fragrant rice from Thailand. But you can also use another long-grain or medium-grain rice. Just be sure to have some rice on hand. It's cheap and goes a long way.

Oyster sauce: Full of umami flavor, traditional oyster sauce is made by long-simmering oysters in water and seasonings. These days, many store-bought oyster sauces are made with oyster extract and seasonings, including soy sauce, sugar, and salt. Oyster sauce is versatile in stir-fries and marinades and as a sauce ingredient.

Peanut oil: This oil is practically essential because it has a high smoke point, which means it can withstand the high heat of wok cooking. It also gives a nice, nutty flavor to food. You can use vegetable oil if you don't have peanut oil. It might be labeled groundnut oil at the grocery store.

All About Soy Sauce

One of the oldest condiments in the world, soy sauce was invented by the Chinese more than 2,500 years ago. It's made from fermented soybeans, wheat, and brine, and now almost all Asian countries use it in their cuisine. There are too many varieties to name, but in Chinese cooking, the two most important types of soy sauce are light and dark.

Light soy sauce is made from the first press of soybeans, and is the one that is most commonly used in Chinese

cooking. It might also be labeled fresh or thin soy sauce at a Chinese grocery, and it is lighter in color but saltier in taste than dark soy sauce. Chinese light soy sauce is the most similar to what you'd get in a big chain supermarket and from a major brand, such as Kikkoman. Dark soy sauce is fermented longer, is thicker in texture, and is sweeter in flavor. It's used to add flavor, texture, and color to dishes.

Tamari is a good choice for those who are on a gluten-free diet or are sensitive to wheat. It's very similar to traditional soy sauce in that it is made from almost all soybeans, with just a trace of wheat or no added wheat.

Store soy sauce in a cool, dark place (not near the stove). Store it in the refrigerator if you don't use it often. You may find you use it in non-Asian cooking as well, such as in chili or barbecue sauce.

Rice vinegar: There are many different types of rice vinegars in China, but get at least one for your dressings and pickles. Made from fermented rice, it's milder and sweeter than Western vinegar.

Shaoxing rice wine: This beverage is both for drinking and for cooking Chinese dishes. Shaoxing rice wine is made from sticky rice, and it adds an unmistakable and pleasant flavor to meat dishes. If you can't find it, use a good dry sherry instead.

Soy sauce (light and dark): There's a good chance you already have soy sauce in your pantry. Chinese cooks use two different types of soy sauce. Light Chinese soy sauce is thinner, clearer, and saltier than dark soy sauce. It's the one most commonly used in cooking, and is similar to the soy sauce you will get in a mainstream grocery store. Light soy sauce might also be labeled as "thin." Dark soy sauce is a little thicker, sweeter, and not as salty as light soy sauce.

Toasted sesame oil: This is a Chinese pantry pick because you can use it to impart a nutty, fragrant flavor to your dishes. A tiny bit goes a long way, so remember to use just a small amount for flavor.

THE BRILLIANT

These are the ingredients that will take your Chinese cooking to the next level. Some, but not all, of these ingredients might be challenging to find. It is definitely worth a trip to an Asian market to try the different varieties that are available.

Black bean sauce: A rich sauce made from fermented black beans and other seasonings, such as garlic and soy sauce. If you buy the sauce, then you have a ready-made stir-fry sauce that will transform everyday ingredients. You can also find fermented black beans in Chinese markets and try making your own sauce.

Bok choy: You can make your stir-fries with peppers, Western onions, and American cabbage with delicious results. But add a traditional Chinese vegetable into the mix, and you won't have leftovers. Bok choy is a type of petite

What's the Deal with MSG?

MSG (monosodium glutamate) is a flavor enhancer used in Chinese and other Asian cuisines, canned soups and vegetables, and processed foods. It's controversial, so you'll often see Asian sauces, foods, and take-out menus stamped with the label No MSG or MSG-Free. The Food and Drug Administration (FDA) has classified MSG as safe to eat, but the FDA also requires MSG to be listed on food labels.

MSG's ability to enhance flavors was discovered by Japanese scientist Kikunae Ikeda in 1908. He was researching seaweed and why it makes food taste better. His research found that an amino acid called L-glutamate is responsible. This amino acid occurs naturally in many places, including meat, vegetables, and dairy products.

When sodium is added to glutamate, it becomes a salt, which is what Ikeda did to make it easy to use glutamate in the kitchen.

Many scientists, food companies, and the FDA believe that MSG is totally safe to eat. But there are countless anecdotal complaints about what consumers call MSG complex or Chinese restaurant syndrome. The symptoms include headache, sweating, numbness or tingling, chest pain, lethargy, and nausea.

Despite all the research, it is still unknown why some people don't feel well after eating Chinese take-out. Some scientists don't believe MSG is the culprit, because the same symptoms aren't reported when people eat non-Chinese foods that contain more MSG than the average Chinese take-out meal. Some researchers believe the combination of overeating, drinking alcohol, excessive amounts of sodium and fat, and various other factors paired with eating Chinese take-out is the culprit. But if you feel one or some of these symptoms after enjoying Chinese take-out, test the theory by cooking some of the recipes in this cookbook at home—using MSG-free sauces, of course.

cabbage, and it's simple to cook and good in stir-fries, salads, and soups. Buy baby bok choy if possible, or at least the smallest one you can find.

Chinkiang black rice vinegar: A specialty vinegar, this black rice vinegar has an unmistakable earthy, smoky flavor. Like balsamic vinegar, the taste is distinctive when it's used in cooking and in sauces. If you're unable to find it, use a good quality balsamic vinegar instead.

Dried mushrooms: You can and should buy fresh mushrooms, but having a couple of different types of dried mushrooms (such as shiitakes) in your pantry will make cooking easier, especially if it's spur-of-the-moment. Rehydrate dried mushrooms in water, and add them to stir-fries, soups, and meat dishes.

Sichuan peppercorns: These small pods are also known as Chinese coriander, Szechuan pepper, Chinese prickly ash, flower pepper, and lemon pepper. They are used all over Asia and are not spicy. They have a lemon flavor that adds essential seasoning and aroma to meats, fish, and vegetables. They also create a tingle in the mouth.

Spicy bean sauce: Also called spicy bean paste or *toban jiang* or *toban dian*, spicy bean sauce adds an unmistakable umami flavor to your dishes. It's important in Sichuan (Szechuan) cuisine and is made of fermented beans, oil, and chiles.

Tofu: You can add tofu to soups, stews, salads, stir-fries, and main dishes. You can now buy boxed tofu that lasts for quite a while in your pantry. It's inexpensive and a great meat substitute for vegetarians. The type of tofu used depends on what you're making. Firm and extra-firm tofu holds its form in stir-fries, whereas soft and medium tofu is used in dishes such as Mapo Tofu (page 127), where it breaks apart and becomes part of a bubbling stew.

ESSENTIAL COOKING TOOLS

Besides your wok, there are some cooking tools that will make everyday and Chinese cooking easier. If you already cook, then you might already have what you need, including a wooden spoon, tongs, and a bamboo steamer.

Bamboo steamer: With a bamboo steamer, you can make dumplings, steamed fish, and other delicate dishes in your wok. If you get a multilayer steamer, you can steam by layers, according to how much time the different foods need to be steamed. If you're planning to steam often, then get a steamer that's large, ideally 8 to 10 inches in diameter.

Rice cooker: If you cook any type of Asian food or grain, then a rice cooker is a real time-saver. It keeps rice and grains warm and ready for as long as a couple of days. A wok and a rice cooker make delicious 15-minute dinners possible.

Tongs or cooking chopsticks: Using tongs or cooking chopsticks makes moving things around easy. Cooking chopsticks are long and heat-resistant, so get these if you're already good at using chopsticks. If not, tongs will do the trick. You'll be surprised at how useful cooking chopsticks are in the kitchen.

ORIGIN STORIES | *Egg Drop Soup*

Just like most Chinese American dishes, the egg drop soup we enjoy stateside is based on a Chinese dish. This one is called egg flower soup in China. The "flower" refers to the strands of egg, which create wispy flowers in the broth. To achieve the perfect thin strands, cooks must gently pour beaten egg into a simmering chicken broth.

American egg drop soup is similar to the original in that it is swirled egg cooked in chicken broth, but it is different in both consistency and color. The version we are used to is extremely thick and usually a neon-yellow color. The thickness comes from cornstarch, which is added to the broth, and the bright hue commonly comes from food coloring.

Although thickeners for sauce and soup are used in traditional Chinese cuisines, they are used much more liberally in American-style Chinese cooking. Hot and sour soup, another popular Chinese take-out soup, also has a much thicker consistency than its traditional Chinese counterpart.

Wide spatula: The wide metal wok spatula is the thing to use for fried rice to make sure you can scrape up anything sticky while cooking. But for most stir-fries and other dishes, you can use a regular wide-angled wooden or metal spatula.

Wide strainer or slotted spoon: Bamboo strainers are traditional in Chinese restaurants, but you can use any good-quality hand-held strainer or slotted spoon for frying or draining food such as dumplings.

Wok lid: Inexpensive and light, this is necessary for braising and steaming. If you intend to do a lot of braising, buy a domed or flat lid that fits your wok.

Wooden spoons: Use wooden spoons to stir-fry, stir, and move food around your wok. They are heat resistant and won't scrape the surface of your seasoned wok.

3 | DUMPLINGS, EGG ROLLS, AND DIM SUM FAVORITES

Scallion Pancakes

MAKES 4 | PREP TIME: 40 MINUTES | COOK TIME: 10 MINUTES

Under $10 • Vegan   These flaky savory "pancakes" are one of the most popular dim sum dishes. With just a few ingredients needed, they are simple to make at home. Try your hand at making these crispy appetizers for your next dinner or party. They'll disappear as quickly as you can make them.

2 cups all-purpose flour, plus additional for dusting

¾ cup warm water

½ cup cold water

2 to 4 tablespoons vegetable or peanut oil, plus additional as needed

3 or 4 scallions, thinly sliced

Time-Saving Tip: You can freeze the scallion dough if you prepare it in advance. Just separate the layers of dough with parchment paper.

1. In a large bowl, mix the flour and warm water together to form a dough. Work the cold water into the dough, a little bit at a time, until a smooth and not too sticky dough forms.

2. On a clean work surface, knead the dough for 10 minutes. If the dough seems too sticky at first, dust the work surface with a little flour. The dough will become smoother the more it is kneaded, and extra flour should not be necessary. Place the dough back in the bowl, and cover it with a damp cloth or paper towel. Let the dough rest for 30 minutes.

3. Roll out the dough onto a floured cutting board. Divide it into four equal pieces.

4. Roll each piece of dough into a level circle, 7 to 8 inches in diameter. Brush the top of each circle lightly with some of the oil. Top each circle with one quarter of the scallions.

5. Fold the edges of the dough over the top of the scallions to create a ball. Then flatten the dough and roll out each again to incorporate the scallions into the dough.

6. Heat your wok over medium-low heat. Using about ½ to 1 tablespoon of oil, lightly fry each dough circle until golden brown, 2 to 3 minutes per side.

7. Serve warm with Sesame Dipping Sauce (page 134) or regular soy sauce.

Perfect Pork Pot Stickers

SERVES 4 AS AN APPETIZER | PREP TIME: 35 MINUTES | COOK TIME: 10 MINUTES

This is a straightforward recipe for classic Chinese pork pot stickers, the crowd-pleasing appetizer, main dish, or snack. Using pork in the filling makes soft dumplings like the kind you'd get from your favorite take-out place.

1. Put the cabbage in a strainer in the sink or over a bowl, and sprinkle it with the kosher salt. Mix the kosher salt with the cabbage to coat the cabbage. Let the cabbage sit for 15 minutes. Using your hands, squeeze any water from the cabbage, getting as much out as possible.

2. In a medium bowl, mix together the cabbage, ginger, scallions, pork, white pepper, soy sauce, rice wine, and sesame oil. Using your hands, mix the ingredients thoroughly until they are sticky.

3. To make each dumpling, place a packed tablespoon of filling in the center of a wrapper. Wet your finger and trace the entire edge of the wrapper to dampen it. Fold the wrapper in half, and press the wet edges together. Pinch the edges to create small pleats. Repeat this for all the wrappers.

4. Heat a wok to medium-high, and add the peanut oil. Place the pot stickers into the wok, seam-side up. Cook the dumplings for about 1 minute, until the bottoms are golden brown.

5. Add the warm water to the wok. Cover the wok and cook the pot stickers for 7 to 8 minutes, or until the water has boiled off.

6. Remove the wok from the heat.

7. Serve warm with your favorite hot chili sauce or dumpling dipping sauce.

12 ounces napa cabbage leaves, chopped

1 teaspoon kosher salt

1 teaspoon grated fresh ginger

¼ cup minced scallions

1 pound ground pork

⅛ teaspoon white pepper

1½ tablespoons soy sauce

1 tablespoon Shaoxing rice wine

2 teaspoons toasted sesame oil

30 to 40 dumpling wrappers (*gyoza*, pot sticker, or *mandu*)

1½ tablespoons peanut or vegetable oil

¼ cup water, room temperature or warm

Ingredient Tip: Feel free to use green cabbage if you don't have napa.

HOW TO
Fold a Pot Sticker or Dumpling

1 Hold the wrapper in one hand and place 1 tablespoon of filling in the center of the wrapper. Wet your finger and trace the entire edge of the wrapper to dampen it.

2 Gently fold the wrapper in half, but do not seal the edges together.

3 Use your right thumb and index finger to make a small pleat in the top layer of the wrapper, leaving the bottom layer un-pleated. Press the pleated layer together with the un-pleated layer. Repeat 5 to 6 times.

4 Run your fingers along the edges of the wrapper together to ensure that the pot sticker or dumpling is completely sealed.

Shrimp and Beef Pot Stickers

SERVES 4 | PREP TIME: 35 MINUTES | COOK TIME: 10 MINUTES

These dumplings are big in taste and a snap to put together. In American-style Chinese restaurants, the pot stickers are usually made with pork, but beef and lamb are also typical dumpling fillings in northern China. This is a great recipe to experiment with other filling ingredients, such as chicken, pork, turkey, and tofu.

1. Finely chop the shrimp or process it in a food processor. Set it aside.

2. Finely chop the ground beef by running a knife through it so it is in small chunks.

3. In a large bowl, mix the shrimp and beef with the ginger, shallot, cabbage, soy sauce, and sesame oil. Season with the salt and pepper. Continue mixing until well combined.

4. To make each dumpling, place a packed tablespoon of filling in the center of a wrapper. Wet your finger and trace the entire edge of the wrapper to dampen it. Fold the wrapper in half, and press the wet edges together. Pinch the edges to create small pleats. Repeat this for all the wrappers.

5. Heat your wok over medium heat, add the vegetable oil to it, and then add the dumplings, seam-side up, for about 2 minutes, or until they are golden brown on the bottom. Pour the water over the dumplings. Cover the wok with a lid, and let the dumplings steam for 5 to 6 minutes.

6. Uncover the wok and let the dumplings cook for another 2 minutes, or until the water has boiled off.

½ **pound raw shrimp, peeled and deveined**

2 **pounds ground beef**

1½ **teaspoons minced fresh ginger**

1 **shallot, minced**

2 **leaves napa cabbage, chopped**

1½ **tablespoons soy sauce**

¾ **teaspoon toasted sesame oil**

Salt

Freshly ground black pepper

30 **to** 40 **round pot sticker, dumpling, or** *gyoza* **wrappers**

1½ **tablespoons vegetable or peanut oil**

½ **cup water, at room temperature or warm**

Cooking Tip: Once you make and fill these dumplings, you can also boil, steam, or deep-fry them in your wok.

Succulent Shrimp Wontons

SERVES 4 | PREP TIME: 25 MINUTES | COOK TIME: 10 MINUTES

Nut-free   These wontons are easy to make, and once you make them, you can quickly fry them in your wok as an appetizer, use them in a wonton soup, or steam them and serve them with a spicy chili sauce. Once you know how to assemble these, you can experiment with different fillings.

⅓ pound raw, peeled shrimp, washed and deveined, with tails removed

½ teaspoon sesame oil

Salt

Freshly ground white pepper

14 to 20 wonton wrappers

1 egg, beaten

Cooking Tip: Instead of creating triangles, you can gather the wonton wrapper edges together at the top of the filling, so that each wrapper is a little rectangular package.

1. Chop the shrimp into a fine mince, and mix it with the sesame oil. Season with the salt and white pepper.

2. Place a teaspoon of the filling in the center of each wonton wrapper. Brush the edges of the wonton wrappers with the beaten egg.

3. Fold the wontons to make triangles. Press the edges together. Let the wontons dry for about 10 minutes. Place the wontons in a steamer basket in a single layer.

4. Fill the wok with 2 inches of water, and bring it to a boil. Turn the heat down to a simmer, and place the steamer basket in the wok. Cover the wok and let the wontons steam for 6 to 8 minutes.

5. Serve with a spicy dipping sauce or chili-garlic sauce.

Easy Egg and Scallion Dumplings

SERVES 4 | PREP TIME: 5 MINUTES | COOK TIME: 15 MINUTES

Under $10 • *Quick & Easy* • *Vegetarian*   The eggs and scallions in this recipe give it great flavor. After you whip up a batch of these, you can prepare them however you wish, whether it's steaming, frying, boiling, or using them in soup. These dumplings are healthy, protein packed, and delicious. If you want something completely different, you can even throw a little cheese into these to make a breakfast-style dumpling.

1. To a hot wok, add the vegetable oil and sesame oil. Add the garlic and cook for about 30 seconds.

2. Add the eggs to the wok, and season with the sea salt and pepper. Scramble the eggs with a heat-proof spatula for about 30 seconds, or until done. Add the scallions and mix with the scrambled eggs. Transfer the eggs to a plate, and set aside to cool until they can be handled.

3. Spoon a heaping teaspoon of the egg and scallion filling into the center of a dumpling wrapper. Wet the edges of the wrapper with water, fold the wrapper to enclose the filling, and seal the dumpling by pinching the wrapper at its edges. Repeat with the remaining wrappers and filling. Make sure the uncooked dumplings don't touch each other. They will stick together until they're cooked.

4. Steam, pan-fry, boil, or deep-fry the dumplings, or use them in soup.

2 tablespoons vegetable or peanut oil

½ teaspoon toasted sesame oil

1 teaspoon minced garlic

4 large eggs, beaten

Sea salt

Freshly ground black pepper

2 scallions, trimmed and chopped

24 to 30 dumpling, *gyoza*, or pot sticker wrappers

Time-Saving Tip: If you're making a big batch of these dumplings to freeze, do so in a single layer, making sure they don't touch. Once frozen, you can transfer them to resealable freezer bags. You can fry, steam, or boil these straight from the freezer without defrosting.

HOW TO
Fold an Egg Roll

1   Place the wrapper on a clean surface with one point facing you. Spread 1 tablespoon of the filling on the wrapper in a horizontal line slightly closer to you.

2   Roll the point of the wrapper closer to you over the filling.

3   Fold in the two side corners of the wrapper.

4   Dampen the remaining open point of the wrapper with water. Finish rolling the egg roll away from you.

Vegetable Egg Rolls

SERVES 4 | PREP TIME: 25 MINUTES | COOK TIME: 10 MINUTES

Under $10 • Vegan   American-style egg rolls are deep-fried and crispy. You can re-create the flavor and crispness of these egg rolls by wok-frying this vegetable version. They're still delicious but a lot healthier and less oily than take-out egg rolls.

1. To a hot wok over medium-high heat, add 1 teaspoon of peanut oil, the garlic, and the ginger, and stir-fry for about 30 seconds. Add the onion, celery, and carrots to the wok, and stir-fry for about 2 minutes. Add the cabbage, rice vinegar, soy sauce, and sugar. Stir-fry the mixture for another 2 minutes. Remove the vegetables from the wok, and let them cool until they can be handled.

2. Place the egg roll wrappers on a clean surface with a point facing you. Spread 1 tablespoon of the filling in a horizontal line, slightly closer to you. Roll the point of the wrapper closest to you over the filling. Fold in the two side corners. Dampen the remaining open point with water, and finish rolling the egg roll away from you.

3. The egg rolls will be fried in two batches. To a wok over medium-high heat, add 1 tablespoon of the peanut oil. Place the egg rolls in the wok, seam-side down. Fry them for about 5 to 8 minutes, turning often so they cook evenly. Repeat this step with the rest of the egg rolls.

4. Serve with plum sauce, sweet and sour sauce, chili sauce, or duck sauce.

2 tablespoons plus 1 teaspoon peanut oil, divided

2 garlic cloves, minced

1 tablespoon minced fresh ginger or ⅓ teaspoon ground ginger

½ sweet onion, thinly sliced

1 celery stalk, thinly sliced

2 carrots, cut into matchsticks

½ small cabbage, shredded

2 tablespoons rice vinegar

2 teaspoons soy sauce

1 teaspoon sugar

40 to 50 egg roll wrappers

Ingredient Tip: To make more traditional egg rolls, add 1 pound of bean sprouts to the vegetable mix. Make sure to wash the bean sprouts well and thoroughly dry them.

HOW TO
Fold a Wonton

1 Place the wonton wrapper on a clean surface with one point facing you. In the center of the wonton wrapper, place 1 teaspoon of the filling.

2 Dampen the edges of the wonton wrapper with water. Fold over the edges of the wrapper to make a triangle. Ensure that the edges are sealed.

3 Pull in the two side points of the triangle together so that one overlaps the other. Press them together to ensure that they are sealed.

Quick-Fried Wontons at Home

SERVES 4 | PREP TIME: 30 MINUTES | COOK TIME: 10 MINUTES

Under $10   Deep-fried wontons are one of those things everyone loves. Just like with the other wonton and dumpling recipes in this chapter, you can also pan-fry or steam these. But this recipe shows you how to deep-fry them if you want to make them restaurant-style. For a different take, drop a few deep-fried wontons into a simple soup broth. The dough becomes chewy, the broth becomes rich, and the result is delicious.

1. In a large bowl, mix together the pork, garlic, ginger, sesame oil, soy sauce, scallions, and carrots.

2. In the center of a wonton wrapper, place about a teaspoon of the pork filling. Dampen the edges of the wonton wrapper with a little water, and fold the edges over to make a triangle. Using your fingers, press the edges together to seal the wonton.

3. To a wok, add enough of the peanut oil so that it is about 1½ inches deep. Heat the oil to 350°F. Fry 5 or 6 wontons at a time until they're golden brown. Continue until all are fried.

4. Drain the finished wontons on a rack or a plate covered with paper towels. Serve with chili sauce or sweet and sour sauce.

1 pound ground pork

2 garlic cloves, minced

1 teaspoon minced fresh ginger

1 teaspoon toasted sesame oil

1 tablespoon soy sauce

5 scallions, finely chopped

2 carrots, finely chopped

40 to 50 wonton wrappers

Peanut oil, for deep-frying

Healthy Tip: For lighter wontons, you can skip the deep-frying. Instead, bake them in a preheated 400°F oven for 7 to 10 minutes, or until golden brown.

Wonton Soup

SERVES 4 | PREP TIME: 25 MINUTES | COOK TIME: 10 MINUTES

Nut-free • Under $10 • Quick & Easy   This is simple, classic wonton soup in a clear chicken broth. You can use homemade wontons and homemade chicken broth for a fantastic flavor, or you can make a delicious, 15-minute soup with frozen chicken or pork wontons and good-quality chicken broth.

6 cups chicken broth, homemade or store-bought

12 to 15 wontons [such as Succulent Shrimp Wontons (page 38) or Quick-Fried Wontons at Home (page 43)]

1 scallion, finely chopped

1. In your wok, bring the chicken broth to a boil. Carefully add the wontons, one at a time; lower the heat to a simmer. The wontons are ready when they float to the top of the broth.

2. Spoon the soup into individual bowls, and garnish with the chopped scallion.

Simple Shanghai Buns

SERVES 4 | PREP TIME: 40 MINUTES | COOK TIME: 15 MINUTES

Nut-free • *Under $10*   These steamed dumplings are a simplified but still super tasty version of Shanghai dumplings. With just a few ingredients, you can make these cute little bundles. These can be a meal by themselves or accompany a larger dinner.

1. To make the dough, mix together the flour, yeast, baking powder, and sugar in a medium mixing bowl. Let the dough rest for 30 minutes.

2. In a large bowl, mix the cabbage, ground beef, soy sauce, and sesame oil together.

3. Once the dough has rested, divide it into 15 equal pieces. Roll a dough piece into a circle, about 4 inches in diameter. Put about 1 tablespoon of filling in the center of the dough circle. Bring the edges of the dough together at the top, and twist and pinch them together to seal. Repeat this for the remaining dough pieces and the filling.

4. Add about 2 inches of water to your wok. Place a piece of parchment paper in the bottom of a bamboo steamer, and put the steamer in the wok. Bring the water to a boil.

5. Place the buns in the bamboo steamer, making sure they do not touch. Cover the steamer and steam the buns until they are cooked, about 15 minutes.

6. Serve with black vinegar or your favorite dumpling dipping sauce on the side.

2 cups all-purpose flour

2 teaspoons yeast

2 teaspoons baking powder

2 teaspoons sugar

½ cup chopped napa cabbage

1½ pounds lean ground beef

2 tablespoons soy sauce

1 teaspoon toasted sesame oil

Black vinegar (for dipping)

Ingredient Tips: Add ginger and chopped scallions to your filling mix for an even more flavorful, aromatic dumpling. Swap out the ground beef for ground chicken, pork, or chopped shrimp to create a variety of dumplings. Make a vegetarian version of these with drained tofu.

Pork *Shumai*

SERVES 4 | PREP TIME: 50 MINUTES | COOK TIME: 15 MINUTES

Nut-free   *Shumai* are popular in dim sum restaurants, and they are simple to make at home because, unlike dumplings, you don't have to seal them. Although commonly made with shrimp and pork, these pork *shumai* are easier to put together and have a lovely flavor.

FOR THE DIPPING SAUCE

3 tablespoons soy sauce

1 tablespoon chili sauce

1 teaspoon sesame oil

FOR THE FILLING

2 tablespoons soy sauce

2 tablespoons sherry wine

1½ teaspoons sesame oil

2 teaspoons sugar

½ teaspoon salt

1½ teaspoons grated fresh ginger

4 scallions, chopped

3 garlic cloves, minced

2 shiitake mushrooms, chopped

Freshly ground black pepper

1 pound ground pork

30 to 40 wonton wrappers

Ingredient Tip: Scallions are an essential part of this filling, but you can add sweet onions, garlic chives, or leeks. If you don't eat pork, substitute ground chicken, ground turkey, finely chopped shrimp, or tofu as the filling base.

TO PREPARE THE DIPPING SAUCE

In a small bowl, whisk together the soy sauce, chili sauce, and sesame oil. Set aside.

TO PREPARE THE FILLING

1. To a large bowl, add the soy sauce, sherry wine, sesame oil, sugar, salt, ginger, scallions, garlic, and mushrooms. Season with the pepper and mix well. Add the pork to the bowl, and mix to combine well.

2. Place 2 tablespoons of filling in the center of a wonton wrapper. Using your fingers, wet the edges of the wrapper with some water. Gather the sides of the wrapper together so that the wrapper pleats, leaving the top open. Gently flatten the bottom so the *shumai* can sit upright. Repeat this step with the rest of the wonton wrappers until all the filling is gone. Refrigerate the *shumai* for about 30 minutes. Leave enough space between each *shumai* so they do not touch each other or they will stick together.

3. Add 1½ cups of water to your wok. Place a piece of parchment paper in the bottom of a bamboo steamer and put the steamer in the wok. Bring the water to a boil.

4. Place the *shumai* in the bamboo steamer, making sure they do not touch. Cover the steamer and steam the *shumai* 8 to 10 minutes, until they are cooked.

5. Serve with chili-soy dipping sauce.

Crab Rangoon

SERVES 4 | PREP TIME: 25 MINUTES | COOK TIME: 10 MINUTES

A popular appetizer in many American-style Chinese restaurants, crab rangoon is a savory dumpling filled with crabmeat and cream cheese. Some accounts say that crab rangoon was first made popular by Trader Vic's, the famous San Francisco Polynesian and tiki-themed restaurant, in 1957. Other food historians trace it to British-occupied Burma at an even earlier date. Either way, it's a nontraditional recipe, which means you can purchase all the ingredients at your local grocery store.

1. To a medium bowl, add the crabmeat, cream cheese, steak sauce, and garlic powder. Mix well.

2. Place about 1 teaspoon of the filling in the center of a wonton wrapper. Moisten the edges of the wrapper with a little water. Fold the wrapper to form a triangle. Take the two outside points of the wrapper, and press them together firmly.

3. Heat the peanut oil in a wok to 375°F. Deep-fry the wontons, a few at a time, until lightly browned, about 2 minutes. Drain the finished wontons on a wire rack or paper towel–lined plate. Serve warm.

½ pound cooked crabmeat or imitation crab, lightly flaked

5 ounces cream cheese (at room temperature)

½ teaspoon steak sauce

½ teaspoon garlic powder or 2 garlic cloves, minced

25 wonton wrappers

3 cups peanut or vegetable oil

Healthy Tip: If you don't want to deep-fry these, they are also very tasty when baked. Place the filled wontons on a nonstick baking tray, and bake in a preheated 425°F oven for 10 minutes, or until nicely browned.

Marbled Tea Eggs

SERVES 4 | PREP TIME: 5 MINUTES | COOK TIME: 2 HOURS

Nut-free • Under $10 • Vegetarian   If you've ever had tea eggs at a dim sum restaurant, then you're familiar with their lovely flavor and fantastic design. In China, they are commonly served at convenience stores and street stalls as a snack. Although they look like they require a lot of work, they actually don't. You create the marbled look by cracking the eggshells after you hard-boil them but before you simmer them in the flavored tea.

8 eggs

2 black tea bags

½ cup soy sauce

2 teaspoons sugar

2 pieces star anise

1 cinnamon stick

2 thin strips of orange peel

Cooking Tip: For a spicier flavor, you can add 4 whole cloves and 1 teaspoon peppercorns to the flavoring liquid.

1. In a medium pot, cover the eggs with water. Bring the water to a boil, and then immediately turn the heat down to a simmer. Cook the eggs for about 10 minutes, until hard-boiled.

2. Remove the eggs from the pot, and cool them under cold running water.

3. Using the back of a spoon, crack the eggs evenly all around, making sure not to peel off the shells.

4. Return the eggs to the pot, and add the tea bags, soy sauce, sugar, star anise, cinnamon stick, and orange peel. Add enough water to the pot to cover the eggs.

5. Bring the water to a boil, and then immediately lower the heat. Simmer the eggs for 40 minutes. Turn off the heat, cover the pot with a lid, and then let the eggs steep for at least 1 hour. The longer you steep the eggs, the stronger the flavor and color will be.

6. Drain the eggs. Serve immediately as a snack or with noodles or rice.

Mango Pudding

SERVES 4 | PREP TIME: 5 MINUTES | CHILLING TIME: 2 HOURS

Gluten-free • Nut-free • Under $10   Chinese cuisine does not include many desserts. This mango pudding was created in a rapidly developing Hong Kong in the 1950s, when canned foods were imported and quickly became integrated into local cooking. This cold, creamy mango pudding is delicious and easy to whip up at home.

1. In a blender, purée the mango and sugar until smooth.

2. In a large bowl, mix the hot water and gelatin. Let it stand for a few minutes.

3. Add the evaporated milk to the gelatin, and stir until they are combined. Add the mango purée and mix until well combined.

4. Pour the pudding into individual small cups or ramekins. Cover each one with plastic wrap, and chill in the refrigerator for at least 2 hours.

5. Before serving, garnish each pudding with the raspberries or kiwi (if using).

½ **pound frozen mango chunks**

¼ **cup sugar**

½ **cup hot water**

1 **packet unflavored gelatin**

½ **cup evaporated milk**

Raspberries or kiwi slices, for garnish (optional)

Ingredient Tip: Are you using fresh mangos? Then substitute 2 ripe, peeled mangos for the frozen mangos. If you don't want to use evaporated milk, then substitute ½ cup heavy cream.

4 | VEGETABLES, TOFU, AND EGGS

Spinach with Garlic

SERVES 4 AS A SIDE | PREP TIME: 5 MINUTES | COOK TIME: 5 MINUTES

Gluten-free • Under $10 • Quick & Easy • Vegan   This is a simple, beautiful dish. The flavors of the garlic and spinach stand out, and it's a healthy side that can go with any type of cuisine, from Chinese to American to Italian to you name it.

4 teaspoons peanut or vegetable oil

5 garlic cloves, thinly sliced or crushed

1 (10-ounce) bag raw spinach, washed and drained well

Sea salt

Ingredient Tip: Experiment by adding spices and seasonings, such as chiles, soy sauce, sesame seeds, or sesame oil, to create the dish you want.

1. Heat your wok and add the peanut oil until it begins to smoke.

2. Add the garlic and stir-fry it very briefly, about 10 seconds.

3. Before the garlic begins to burn, quickly add the spinach and stir-fry. The spinach will reduce in size quickly. After a minute or two, once the spinach looks wilted but still bright green, remove it from the wok. Drain off any excess liquid.

4. Season the spinach with the sea salt and serve.

Wok-Seared Broccoli

SERVES 4 | PREP TIME: 5 MINUTES | COOK TIME: 10 MINUTES

Under $10 • *Quick & Easy* • *Vegan*   You can find broccoli all over Chinese menus in America, but the broccoli we eat here looks nothing like Chinese broccoli. If you can find Chinese broccoli (*kai-lan*) or broccolini (a cross between *kai-lan* and broccoli) to use in this recipe, then you'll fall in love with its crisp-tender texture and flavor. It's a cross between bok choy and broccoli.

1. Heat your wok over high heat until a drop of water sizzles on contact. Add the peanut oil and quickly swirl it to coat the wok.

2. Add the broccoli and onion, and toss them in the wok. Reduce the heat to medium-high, and stir-fry the vegetables for a few minutes, allowing parts of the broccoli to brown.

3. Add the chicken broth to the wok and cover it. Cook the broccoli for 2 to 3 minutes longer, until it is crisp-tender.

4. Remove the cover from the wok, and add the soy sauce and orange juice. Season with the sea salt and pepper. Stir-fry the vegetables for 2 to 3 minutes, or until all the liquid has evaporated.

1½ teaspoons peanut or vegetable oil

6 cups broccoli florets (about 2 medium bunches), washed and dried well

½ sweet onion, thinly sliced

1 cup chicken or vegetable broth

2 tablespoons soy sauce

2 teaspoons orange juice

Sea salt

Freshly ground black pepper

Easy Vegetable Stir-Fry

SERVES 4 | PREP TIME: 15 MINUTES | COOK TIME: 10 MINUTES

Under $10 • Quick & Easy • Vegan This is a colorful vegetable stir-fry full of good-for-you vitamins and minerals. You can find almost all of these ingredients at your local grocery, and you can substitute other vegetables you have in your fridge or that you like better. It's a perfect recipe for using whatever you have on hand.

4 tablespoons soy sauce

2 tablespoons sugar

1 tablespoon peanut or vegetable oil

1½ teaspoons grated fresh ginger

1 cup halved cremini or button mushrooms

1 red bell pepper, cut into strips

1 green bell pepper, cut into strips

2 scallions, chopped

1 cup bite-size pieces of broccoli florets

½ cup (trimmed and cut into thirds) green beans

1. In a small bowl, mix the soy sauce and sugar. Set aside.

2. To a wok over medium-high heat, add the peanut oil. Add the ginger and stir-fry it for about 1 minute. Add the mushrooms, red bell pepper, green bell pepper, scallions, broccoli, and green beans. Put a lid on the wok, and cook the vegetables for about 4 minutes. Remove the lid and stir-fry the vegetables for 1 to 2 minutes. Add the sugar and soy sauce mixture, and toss to coat the vegetables. Cook them for about 3 minutes, or until the liquid has cooked off and the vegetables are crisp-tender.

3. Remove the wok from the heat and serve.

Spicy Eggplant with Garlic

SERVES 4 | PREP TIME: 10 MINUTES | COOK TIME: 10 MINUTES

Under $10 • *Quick & Easy*   A popular Sichuan (Szechuan) dish is eggplant cooked with minced pork, chiles, and garlic. The American version is similar but usually has no pork. The important thing here is to try to use thin, long Asian eggplants, not the big, globe eggplants, which are more common in America. Asian eggplants have no bitterness and have a sweeter, more delicate flavor.

1. In a small bowl, mix together the chicken broth, soy sauce, vinegar, brown sugar, chili oil, and red pepper flakes. Set aside.

2. Place a wok over high heat until a drop of water sizzles on contact. Add the peanut oil and swirl to coat the wok.

3. Add the eggplants to the wok, and stir-fry for 2 to 3 minutes, until the outsides become golden brown. Turn down the heat to medium-high, and add the scallions, ginger, and garlic. Stir-fry for about 30 seconds, and then add in the chicken broth mixture; toss the vegetables until they are coated with the sauce. Simmer the vegetables for 2 to 3 minutes, allowing the eggplant to absorb the sauce.

¼ cup chicken broth

1 tablespoon soy sauce

1 tablespoon Chinese black vinegar or good balsamic vinegar

1 tablespoon brown sugar

1 tablespoon chili oil

¼ teaspoon red pepper flakes

2 tablespoons peanut or vegetable oil

2 to 3 Asian eggplants, cut into thin, 1-inch-long strips

2 scallions, minced

1 tablespoon fresh minced ginger

2 garlic cloves, minced

Dry-Fried Green Beans

SERVES 4 | PREP TIME: 5 MINUTES | COOK TIME: 8 MINUTES

Under $10 • *Quick & Easy* This dish, done right, is fragrant and flavorful. Don't be afraid to let the green beans blister with the high heat, and feel free to add some chili sauce or chile peppers to the mix if you want to spice things up.

¼ cup peanut or vegetable oil

1 pound string beans, trimmed and completely dry

1 clove garlic, crushed

2 tablespoons oyster sauce

1 teaspoon Shaoxing rice wine

3 scallions, thinly sliced

1. Place your wok over high heat. When it is hot, add the peanut oil. Add the string beans to the wok, and cook them until they are crinkly and blistered, tossing them continuously for about 5 minutes. Remove the beans from the wok.

2. Keeping the wok over high heat, add the crushed garlic, oyster sauce, rice wine, and scallions to the wok and stir-fry until fragrant, about 30 seconds. Return the green beans to the wok, and toss them in the sauce until they are coated. Stir-fry the beans for 1 minute. Serve hot.

Bok Choy with Garlic

SERVES 4 | PREP TIME: 10 MINUTES | COOK TIME: 5 MINUTES

Under $10 • Quick & Easy • Vegan   A vegetable native to China, bok choy has a great, crunchy texture and fresh flavor. It's part of the cabbage family. If you can get to an Asian grocery store, you can purchase very small bok choy—sometimes called baby bok choy—which is delicious and wonderfully tender. If you're shopping at a non-Asian market, select the smallest bunch.

1. Trim the root ends of the baby bok choy. Wash and thoroughly drain the leaves.

2. Heat your wok to medium-high; add the peanut oil and swirl to coat the wok. Add the garlic and ginger, and cook them for 30 seconds to 1 minute. Do not let them burn. When the spices become fragrant, add the bok choy leaves. Stir-fry everything together until well combined.

3. Add the vegetable broth to the wok. Cover the wok and cook for about 1 minute. Remove the cover from the wok, and turn off the heat. Season the bok choy with the sea salt, drizzle it with the sesame oil, and toss to coat. Serve immediately.

1½ **pounds baby bok choy**

1½ **tablespoons peanut or vegetable oil**

1 **or 2 garlic cloves, minced**

¼ **teaspoon ground ginger**

3 **tablespoons vegetable broth**

Sea salt

½ **teaspoon toasted sesame oil**

Chinese Steamed Eggs

SERVES 4 | PREP TIME: 5 MINUTES | COOK TIME: 20 MINUTES

Nut-free • Under $10 • Quick & Easy • Vegetarian   This is a traditional Chinese dish often seen in dim sum and Chinese restaurants in America. On the menu it is sometimes called egg custard. It's usually a velvety smooth egg side dish, but you can also make it for breakfast if you're looking for a new way to make eggs.

3 medium eggs

2 teaspoons sea salt

1 cup water

Soy sauce

Sesame oil

1 scallion, finely chopped

1. In a large bowl, beat the eggs. Pour the eggs through a sieve into a steam-proof dish. Add the sea salt to the dish, and whisk it into the eggs.

2. In your wok over high heat, bring the water to a boil. Place a steamer rack or colander with legs in the wok. Carefully place the dish with the eggs in the wok, and cover the dish with a heat-proof plate. Turn the heat to low, and steam the eggs for 15 minutes.

3. Carefully remove the dish. Serve the eggs with soy sauce and sesame oil and garnished with a chopped scallion.

Hot and Sour Vegetable Soup

SERVES 4 | PREP TIME: 10 MINUTES | COOK TIME: 20 MINUTES

Nut-free • Quick & Easy   A staple in American Chinese restaurants, hot and sour soup is sometimes unreasonably thick. This recipe still has the spicy and sour flavors of the restaurant-style soup, but it is lighter, with less cornstarch and oil. Feel free to substitute different vegetables and meat. If you want a thicker texture, double the cornstarch.

1. Bring the chicken broth to a simmer in your wok. Add the soy sauce, shredded chicken, shiitake mushrooms, and garlic chili sauce to the broth. Simmer for 3 to 5 minutes. Add the vinegar, pepper, bamboo shoots, and tofu to the wok. Simmer for 5 to 7 minutes more.

2. Add the cornstarch mixture to the soup, and stir the soup to combine. Simmer for about 5 minutes, until the soup has thickened.

3. Slowly pour the egg into the wok in a fine stream. Gently stir the soup a few times. Add the scallions and sesame oil to the soup. Give it a gentle stir and serve.

4 cups chicken or vegetable broth

3 tablespoons soy sauce

¼ cup cooked shredded chicken (or pork)

½ cup shiitake or cremini mushrooms, diced

1 tablespoon garlic chili sauce

¼ cup white vinegar

¼ teaspoon ground pepper

⅓ cup canned bamboo shoots, julienned

3-ounce block of firm tofu, cut into ½-inch-thin strips

1 tablespoon cornstarch mixed with 1 tablespoon cold water

1 egg, beaten

2 scallions, diced

½ teaspoon toasted sesame oil

Egg Drop Soup

SERVES 4 | PREP TIME: 5 MINUTES | COOK TIME: 10 MINUTES

Nut-free • Under $10 • Quick & Easy   This soup is now as much an American comfort food as chicken noodle soup, and it's one of the easiest soups to whip up at home. Unlike the egg drop soup served in most Chinese restaurants, this healthier version is not overly thick or neon yellow.

6 cups chicken broth

1 teaspoon Shaoxing rice wine

¼ teaspoon ground ginger

1 teaspoon sugar

¼ teaspoon ground white pepper

1 tablespoon cornstarch, dissolved in 3 tablespoons water

2 large eggs

Sea salt

1 scallion, green part only, thinly sliced

Cooking Tip: Transform this soup into a heartier meal by adding chicken, pork, or even dumplings or wontons.

1. In your wok, mix together the chicken broth, rice wine, and ginger, and bring to a boil. Reduce the heat to a simmer, and stir in the sugar and white pepper. Stir the cornstarch mixture into the simmering soup, and continue simmering until the soup has thickened a bit.

2. In a small bowl, whisk the eggs lightly with a fork. Slowly stream the beaten egg into the soup, and keep gently stirring the soup while the egg is being added. The egg will form silky strands in the soup.

3. Turn off the heat immediately, and season the soup with the sea salt. Ladle the soup into individual bowls. Garnish with the thinly sliced scallion and serve.

Vinegar-Glazed Chinese Cabbage

SERVES 4 | PREP TIME: 10 MINUTES | COOK TIME: 5 MINUTES

Under $10 • Quick & Easy • Vegan   This is a simple recipe with tons of flavor. Cabbage is popular all over Asia and is used extensively in Chinese cuisine because it is versatile, healthy, easy to prepare, and inexpensive.

1. In a small bowl, mix the cornstarch and cold water to make a smooth paste. Set aside.

2. To a hot wok, add the peanut oil, and then add the garlic and stir-fry it for about 10 seconds. Before the garlic begins to burn, add the cabbage and stir-fry it for about 2 minutes, or until it has softened completely. Add the vinegar to the wok. Season the cabbage mixture with sea salt, and stir-fry until the vinegar and sea salt have combined with the mixture, about 15 seconds.

3. Add the cornstarch mixture to the wok, and stir-fry for 30 seconds or less, until the sauce has thickened. Remove the wok from the heat and serve.

1 tablespoon cornstarch

2 tablespoons cold water

4 tablespoons peanut oil

3 garlic cloves, very thinly sliced

1 small napa cabbage, washed and shredded

3 tablespoons black vinegar

Sea salt

Ingredient Tip: Can't find napa cabbage or black vinegar near you? Substitute green cabbage for the napa cabbage in this recipe and a good quality balsamic vinegar for the black vinegar.

Lighter Egg Foo Young

SERVES 4 | PREP TIME: 10 MINUTES | COOK TIME: 10 MINUTES

Quick & Easy   Like many American-style Chinese dishes, egg foo young is based on an actual Chinese omelet. But because it was most popular during the chop suey era of Chinese take-out, we know it here only as a tasty but oily and sometimes gloppy dish. This recipe is a lighter-style egg foo young that makes a satisfying breakfast, lunch, or dinner.

FOR THE GRAVY

¾ cup chicken broth

1½ tablespoons hoisin sauce

1 tablespoon cornstarch dissolved in 2 tablespoons cold water

FOR THE EGG FOO YOUNG

3 to 3½ tablespoons peanut or vegetable oil, divided

3 or 4 shiitake or cremini mushrooms, thinly sliced

4 scallions, thinly sliced

1½ cups fresh bean sprouts

¼ cup chopped ham or Canadian bacon

1½ teaspoons soy sauce

1 teaspoon sesame oil

6 large eggs

Healthy Tip: If you don't want to use the gravy, then try some chili sauce or sriracha on your egg foo young.

TO PREPARE THE GRAVY

In a small saucepan, bring the chicken broth to a boil, and then reduce the heat to a simmer. Stir in the hoisin sauce and cornstarch mixture. Simmer the gravy for about 1 minute, and then turn off the heat. Cover the pan.

TO PREPARE THE EGG FOO YOUNG

1. Heat a wok over medium-high heat until a drop of water sizzles on contact. Add 1 tablespoon of peanut oil, and swirl to coat the bottom of the wok.

2. Add the shiitake mushrooms, scallions, and bean sprouts to the wok, and stir-fry them for about 3 minutes. Add the ham, soy sauce, and sesame oil to the wok, and stir-fry them for another 1 to 2 minutes. Remove the filling mixture from the wok and set it aside.

3. In a medium bowl, beat the eggs. Add the filling mixture to the eggs and mix to combine.

4. Heat the wok to medium-high, and add 1 tablespoon of peanut oil. Pour in one quarter of the egg mixture to make an omelet. Cook the egg mixture until it is golden brown, 1 to 2 minutes per side. Transfer the omelet to a plate. Repeat this step with the rest of the egg mixture to make a total of 4 omelets. For each subsequent omelet, use only 1½ teaspoons or less of the remaining peanut oil.

5. To serve, pour some gravy over each omelet.

Mu Shu Vegetables with Steamed Pancakes

SERVES 4 | PREP TIME: 15 MINUTES | COOK TIME: 10 MINUTES

Quick & Easy • Vegetarian   The mu shu dishes Americans love are based on a northern Chinese dish made of pork, eggs, wood ear mushrooms, day lily buds, and bamboo shoots. When it made its way to America, cooks started using American ingredients, such as green cabbage, bell peppers, onions, and celery in their recipes. In China, mu shu dishes are served with rice and noodles; in America, they're served with wraps or tortillas to enjoy taco-style. Because the vegetables in mu shu dishes are shredded, this recipe calls for prebagged coleslaw to make meal prep stress-free.

1. Heat a wok over medium-high heat until it is hot. Add 1 tablespoon of peanut oil. When the oil is hot, add the eggs. Season with the sea salt, and stir-fry to scramble the eggs. Remove the eggs to a clean bowl and set aside.

2. Add the remaining 1 tablespoon of peanut oil to the hot wok. When the oil is hot, add the garlic and ginger and stir-fry for 10 seconds. Before they begin to burn, quickly add the shiitake mushrooms and scallions and stir-fry for 1 to 2 minutes.

3. Add the coleslaw mix, carrots, and rice wine to the wok. Cover the wok, reduce the heat to medium, and cook the vegetables for 3 to 4 minutes. Uncover the wok and cook the vegetables until they are crisp-tender.

4. Return the eggs to the wok, and add the soy sauce and cornstarch. Stir-fry to mix everything. Season with additional sea salt and with the pepper.

5. Serve with the steamed Mandarin pancakes and hoisin sauce.

2 tablespoons peanut or vegetable oil, divided

2 large eggs, beaten

Sea salt

3 tablespoons minced garlic

2 tablespoons minced fresh ginger

8 ounces shiitake or cremini mushrooms, or a combination of both, thinly sliced.

4 scallions, green part only, cut into 1-inch sections

1 (10-ounce) package coleslaw mix

1 cup shredded carrots

¼ cup Shaoxing rice wine

3 tablespoons soy sauce

1 teaspoon cornstarch

Freshly ground black pepper

12 to 14 Mandarin pancakes or flour tortillas, steamed for 5 minutes

Hoisin sauce, slightly thinned with warm water

Shredded Potatoes
with Scallions

SERVES 4 | PREP TIME: 15 MINUTES | COOK TIME: 10 MINUTES

Under $10 • *Quick & Easy* • *Vegan*   These delicious, simple potatoes are crispy, flavorful, and a little bit sour from the rich black vinegar. You can substitute half a thinly sliced sweet onion for the scallions, and you can add in thinly sliced red bell pepper or carrots for vibrant color.

2 medium low-starch potatoes (such as red-skinned potatoes), scrubbed

3 tablespoons peanut or vegetable oil

2 or 3 garlic cloves, crushed

2 whole dried chiles (optional)

2 scallions, thinly sliced

1 tablespoon black vinegar

1 tablespoon soy sauce

Healthy Tip: Keep the peels on the potatoes to keep all of their nutrients and vitamins. Just remember to use low-starch potatoes, such as Red Bliss, so that the potato shreds become crispy, not mushy.

1. Cut the potatoes into matchsticks, taking care to make them uniform in size. Soak the potato shreds in cold water for 10 minutes to remove some of their starch. Then drain, rinse, and thoroughly pat them dry.

2. In a hot wok over high heat, heat the peanut oil until it starts to smoke. Add the garlic and chiles (if using), and stir-fry for 15 seconds. Before they begin to burn, add the scallions and stir-fry for about 30 seconds.

3. Add the potatoes to the wok, and stir-fry for 2 to 3 minutes. Then add the black vinegar and toss to combine. Add the soy sauce and stir-fry for another 2 to 3 minutes, or until the potatoes are cooked through.

Simply Seasoned Chinese Broccoli (*Gai lan*)

SERVES 4 AS A SIDE | PREP TIME: 5 MINUTES | COOK TIME: 10 MINUTES

Vegetarian • Under 30 minutes   *Gai lan*, a Chinese vegetable that's also sometimes called Chinese broccoli, is delicious when it's simply seasoned and stir-fried. It tastes like a cross between bok choy and broccoli rabe, and you won't have a hard time finding it in Chinese or Asian grocery stores. However, you can also make this with curly or flat kale, as it is a good flavor and texture replacement. In general, kale goes well in stir-fries, as it can stand up to the high heat of the wok.

1. Boil 1 cup of water in a kettle or small saucepot.

2. Heat your wok over high heat until a drop of water sizzles on contact.

3. Add the oil and then the garlic to the wok and cook for about 15 seconds.

4. Quickly add the Chinese broccoli and stir-fry in the garlic oil.

5. Pour ½ cup of boiling water into the wok and cook for 5 to 6 minutes, or until the broccoli is tender-crisp.

6. Add the soy and oyster sauces to the wok, stir-fry to combine with the broccoli, and heat for about 1 minute.

7. Remove the wok from the heat and add the sesame oil.

8. Mix to combine and serve hot.

2 tablespoons peanut oil

2 garlic cloves, thinly sliced

1 pound Chinese broccoli (*gai lan*), washed and trimmed

2 tablespoons soy sauce

1 tablespoon oyster sauce

1 teaspoon sesame oil

5 | FISH AND SEAFOOD

Clams in Black Bean Sauce

SERVES 4 | PREP TIME: 12 MINUTES (but soaking especially gritty clams could add 2 hours)
COOK TIME: 10 MINUTES

Chinese black bean sauce makes for a meal you can throw together in 15 to 30 minutes. There are countless varieties and most are inexpensive, so visit your local Chinese or Asian grocery to try a few different kinds. You can also start with the black bean sauce you'll probably find at your local chain grocery store.

1½ pounds littleneck or Manila clams, scrubbed and rinsed well

1 tablespoon peanut or vegetable oil

3 garlic cloves, minced

¼ small sweet onion, chopped

1 teaspoon fresh chopped ginger

2 dried red chiles

1 teaspoon black bean sauce

¼ cup room temperature water

1 teaspoon Shaoxing rice wine

1 teaspoon sugar

1. Discard any of the littleneck clams that have broken shells or that have already opened. If the clams seem extra gritty, soak them in salted water for 1 to 2 hours. Rinse them again before cooking.

2. Heat your wok over high heat until a drop of water sizzles on contact, and then add the peanut oil. Quickly add the garlic, onion, ginger, and chiles, and toss for about 30 seconds.

3. Add the black bean sauce and water to the wok. Stir to combine. Then add the clams, rice wine, and sugar. Bring the liquid up to a boil, place a lid on the wok, and cook until the clams open.

4. Serve with rice or over noodles.

Classic Steamed Fish

SERVES 4 | PREP TIME: 10 MINUTES | COOK TIME: 15 MINUTES

Nut-free • Quick & Easy   This will become a favorite way to prepare white fish fillets, as the fish is delicately seasoned and tender. If you go to a Chinese market, you'll see the seafood still alive and swimming, as the Chinese like to use the freshest fish and freshest meat possible. Check in with your supermarket fish counter to get the freshest fish you can find when making this dish.

1. Pat the fish dry with paper towels.

2. In a small bowl, mix together the soy sauce, rice wine, ginger, sliced scallion, and sesame oil. Drizzle the sauce over the fish fillets. Gently place the fish in a bamboo steamer.

3. Add 2 inches of water to your wok, and bring the water to a boil. Place the steamer in the wok, and cover the steamer with its lid. Steam the fish for 7 to 8 minutes, or until the fish is opaque and starts to flake.

4 (4-ounce) white fish fillets, such as flounder, sea bass, or red snapper

2 tablespoons soy sauce

1 tablespoon Shaoxing rice wine or dry sherry

1 tablespoon very finely sliced, peeled fresh ginger

1 tablespoon very finely sliced, scallion, both green and white parts

1 teaspoon toasted sesame oil

Cooking Tip: If you don't have a steamer, you can make this using a heat-proof dish instead.

No-Cook Poached Fish

SERVES 4 | PREP TIME: 10 MINUTES | COOK TIME: 20 MINUTES

Nut-free • Quick & Easy   This no-cook method for poaching fish makes sure you don't overcook the fish, and gives you tender, moist fillets. The only heat added to the fish comes from the boiling water. Make this recipe either sweeter or spicier by adjusting the spices in your sauce.

2 tablespoons cornstarch

2 teaspoons sea salt

1 teaspoon freshly ground
   black pepper

1 pound meaty fish fillet,
   such as tuna or mahi mahi,
   cleaned and cut into even
   pieces

1 tablespoon soy sauce

1 tablespoon honey

1 tablespoon apple cider vinegar

1 teaspoon toasted sesame oil

2 teaspoons chili sauce

1 scallion, julienned, both green
   and white parts

1. Mix the cornstarch with the sea salt and pepper. Dip the fish fillet into the cornstarch mixture, and coat the fish evenly on both sides. Gently place the fish in your wok.

2. Bring water to a boil in another pot or kettle. It needs to be enough water to fully cover the fish in the wok. Once the water comes to a boil, pour it over the fish so that it's completely covered. Tightly cover the wok with a lid or aluminum foil. Poach the fish for 12 to 14 minutes.

3. While the fish is poaching, create the sauce by mixing together the soy sauce, honey, apple cider vinegar, sesame oil, and chili sauce in a small bowl.

4. When the fish is ready, drain it and transfer it to a serving dish, pour the sauce over the fish, and garnish it with the julienned scallion.

Wok-Smoked Salmon

SERVES 4 | PREP TIME: 20 MINUTES | COOK TIME: 20 MINUTES

Nut-free • Under $10   The wok is a versatile tool for stir-frying, poaching, and steaming, but with the addition of a rack or a metal steamer basket, it also makes an excellent smoker. The wok's width makes it simple to work with, and you'll be amazed how easy it is to smoke fish, poultry, or meat. The tea leaves give proteins an aromatic flavor and taste; for something zestier, add citrus peels.

1. In a large bowl, make a marinade by mixing together the soy sauce, rice wine, ginger, and honey. Cut the salmon fillet into 2-inch pieces, and add the pieces to the bowl; toss to coat with the marinade. Let the salmon marinate for 15 minutes.

2. Line your wok with a large piece of aluminum foil, letting the excess foil hang over the edges of the wok. Prepare the smoking layer by mixing together the brown sugar, rice, black tea leaves, and star anise pods in a small bowl. Spread this on the foil in the bottom of your wok.

3. Set a wire rack or a metal steamer basket with little legs on top of the smoking layer. Heat the wok over high heat until the smoking layer begins to smoke, about 5 to 6 minutes. Gently place the marinated salmon on the rack in a single layer, skin-side down. Reserve the marinade to make the sauce for the fish. Reduce the heat to medium-low, cover the wok, and smoke the salmon for about 10 minutes. Turn off the heat and remove the wok from the heat. Do not remove the lid from the wok.

4. Pour the marinade into a small saucepan and bring it to a boil. Remove it from the heat, and slowly add the cornstarch mixture to the marinade, stirring constantly until the sauce thickens.

5. Remove the smoked salmon from the wok, and place on a serving dish. Drizzle it with the sauce and serve with rice.

½ cup soy sauce

¼ cup Shaoxing rice wine

1 tablespoon minced fresh ginger

1 teaspoon honey

1 pound fresh salmon fillet, cleaned and patted dry

4 tablespoons brown sugar

⅓ cup uncooked long-grain rice

¼ cup black tea leaves, such as oolong

2 star anise pods

1 teaspoon cornstarch, mixed with 4 teaspoons cold water

Wok-Seared Scallops

SERVES 4 | PREP TIME: 5 MINUTES | COOK TIME: 10

Quick & Easy   A seafood meal doesn't get any better than these scallops. Always get the freshest scallops available, and you'll have a dish worthy of company and special occasions. Even better? Prep and cooking take less than 20 minutes.

½ stick butter (4 tablespoons), divided

Splash chili oil

24 large scallops, patted dry

Sea salt

Freshly ground black pepper

2 teaspoons peanut oil

½ sweet onion, diced

2 red bell peppers, diced

2 teaspoons hoisin sauce, thinned with 1 teaspoon water

Healthy Tip: If you don't want to use so much butter, use 1 to 2 tablespoons of peanut oil to sear the scallops. The butter does add a nice flavor, so you can add 1 to 2 tablespoons to the wok when the scallops are returned to the wok with the vegetables.

1. Heat your wok over high heat until a drop of water sizzles on contact. Melt 1 to 2 tablespoons of butter with a splash of chili oil in the wok. Working in batches, add the scallops to the wok. The scallops should not crowd each other. Sear the bottoms of the scallops until browned, about 1 minute. Turn the scallops and sear the other sides, about 1 minute. Season the scallops with the sea salt and pepper after you have turned them to sear on the second side. Transfer the finished scallops to a plate, and cover them with foil. Repeat this step until all the scallops are cooked.

2. Over high heat, add the peanut oil to the wok. When the oil is hot, add the onion and peppers, and stir-fry for 2 to 3 minutes. Add the hoisin sauce and toss to coat the vegetables.

3. When the vegetables are done, return the scallops to the wok. Toss them to combine with the vegetables, and remove the wok from the heat. Serve.

Healthier, Faster Salt-and-Pepper Squid

SERVES 4 | PREP TIME: 7 MINUTES | COOK TIME: 5 MINUTES

Quick & Easy   Salt-and-pepper seafood dishes are perennial favorites in many a Chinatown establishment. This version is the easiest and healthiest way to make and enjoy the flavors and texture of this dish at home. With just a handful of ingredients and less than 15 minutes, you can make a dish that's worthy of company or a special occasion.

1. In a small bowl, mix the sea salt, pepper, and Sichuan peppercorns.

2. Heat your wok over high heat until a drop of water sizzles on contact, and then add the peanut oil. Swirl the oil to coat the bottom of the wok. Add the squid and toss it for about 30 seconds. Then sprinkle it with the salt-and-pepper mix. Stir-fry the squid for another minute but no more, as it cooks almost instantly. Overcooked squid has a rubbery texture.

3. Serve immediately with the lemon wedges and chili soy sauce.

½ teaspoon sea salt

½ teaspoon freshly ground black pepper

¼ teaspoon Sichuan peppercorns

1 tablespoon peanut or vegetable oil

1 pound squid, cleaned and cut into rings or 2-inch tentacles

Lemon wedges, for garnish

Chili soy sauce, for garnish

Stir-Fried Squid with Peppers

SERVES 4 | PREP TIME: 12 MINUTES | COOK TIME: 5 MINUTES

Quick & Easy   This quick dish is full of healthy, flavorful ingredients, including ginger, garlic, and chiles. Use fresh squid if you have access to it, but you can also use frozen.

2 tablespoons brown sugar

1 tablespoon soy sauce

1 teaspoon rice vinegar

2 teaspoons fish sauce

2 tablespoons water

1 pound squid, cleaned and cut into rings or 2-inch tentacles

1½ tablespoons peanut or vegetable oil, divided

2 Chinese dried red chiles

2 garlic cloves, minced

1 teaspoon minced ginger

½ sweet onion, thinly sliced

1 red or green bell pepper, cut into strips

Ingredient Tip: If you cannot find Chinese dried red chiles, use Spanish or Mexican dried red chiles instead.

1. In a small bowl, mix together a sauce of the brown sugar, soy sauce, rice vinegar, fish sauce, and water. Set aside.

2. Bring a large pot of water to a boil. Parboil the squid for 10 seconds. Drain it and set aside.

3. Heat a wok on medium-high until it is hot. Add 1 tablespoon of peanut oil to the wok, and then add the chiles, garlic, and ginger. Stir-fry for about 30 seconds until it is fragrant, and then add the sauce. Stir everything for about 30 seconds to prevent it from burning.

4. Add the squid to the wok, and stir-fry for 30 to 40 seconds. Quickly remove the wok from the heat. Don't overcook the squid, which becomes rubbery when overcooked. Transfer the squid and sauce to a plate, reserving 1 tablespoon of the sauce for the vegetables.

5. Heat the wok over medium-high heat. Add the remaining 1½ teaspoons of peanut oil to the wok, and swirl to coat the bottom of the wok. Add the onion, red bell pepper, and reserved sauce to the wok, and stir-fry until the vegetables are crisp-tender, 2 to 3 minutes.

6. Place the vegetables on a plate, and top with the squid. Serve immediately with steamed rice.

Sweet Chili Shrimp

SERVES 4 | PREP TIME: 15 MINUTES | COOK TIME: 5 MINUTES

Quick & Easy   This take-out favorite is fragrant with a lot of flavor layers, but it takes only a few minutes to cook. When making this at home, you can drastically reduce the sugar and cornstarch for a lighter, healthier, gorgeous shrimp dish.

1. Soak the cellophane noodles in hot water for 10 minutes, or until soft. Drain and set aside.

2. In a large bowl, toss the shrimp with the cornstarch, sea salt, and pepper. Let it sit for 5 minutes.

3. In a small bowl, make the sauce by mixing together the soy sauce, honey, rice vinegar, chili sauce, and rice wine. Set the bowl aside.

4. Heat your wok over high heat until a drop of water sizzles on contact. Add the peanut oil and swirl to coat the wok. Add the garlic and ginger, and stir-fry them for about 20 seconds. Add the shrimp and stir-fry them for 2 to 3 minutes, or until they become bright pink.

5. Remove the wok from the heat. Pour the sauce over the shrimp, add the cellophane noodles, and toss to combine everything. Transfer to a plate and serve immediately.

8 ounces cellophane noodles

1 pound shrimp, peeled, cleaned, and deveined

2 teaspoons cornstarch

½ teaspoon sea salt

¼ teaspoon freshly ground black pepper

1 tablespoon soy sauce

1 tablespoon honey

1 tablespoon rice vinegar

2 teaspoons chili sauce

1 tablespoon Shaoxing rice wine or dry sherry

1 tablespoon peanut or vegetable oil

2 teaspoons minced garlic

1 teaspoon minced fresh ginger

Shrimp with Lobster Sauce

SERVES 4 | PREP TIME: 10 MINUTES | COOK TIME: 20 MINUTES

Quick & Easy   This is a classic American-style Chinese dish that is based on a traditional Chinese white sauce that roughly translates as "the sauce that goes with lobster." There is no actual lobster in lobster sauce; the Chinese version usually has black bean sauce and pork. This Americanized version has neither, but it's tasty and simple to whip up. The sauce is delish poured over rice, too.

2 tablespoons peanut or vegetable oil

2 garlic cloves, minced

12 ounces shrimp, peeled, cleaned, and deveined

1 tablespoon Shaoxing rice wine or dry sherry

1½ cups low-sodium chicken broth

½ teaspoon sesame oil

½ teaspoon sugar

½ teaspoon sea salt

Freshly ground white pepper

½ cup peas, fresh or frozen

1 tablespoon cornstarch mixed with 2 tablespoons cold water

1 egg, beaten

1 scallion, chopped

1. Heat your wok over medium-high heat. Add the peanut oil, garlic, and shrimp, and stir-fry for about 20 seconds. Add the rice wine and toss for another 20 seconds. Add the chicken broth, sesame oil, sugar, and sea salt to the wok. Season the mixture with white pepper. Stir in the peas.

2. Bring the mixture to a simmer, and then slowly stir the cornstarch mixture into the sauce. The sauce will thicken as the cornstarch is stirred into it. If the sauce gets too thick, thin it with a little water or broth, and stop adding the cornstarch mixture if there is any left.

3. Slowly add the egg to the wok, creating threads of egg throughout the sauce. Add the chopped scallion to the wok and stir to combine. Cook for about 15 minutes, stirring occasionally. If the sauce becomes too thick, thin it with a little water.

4. Take the wok off the heat, and serve the shrimp and sauce immediately with rice.

Ingredient Tip: Don't have peas? Don't like peas? Substitute sweet corn for them.

Wok-Seared Sea Bass with Ginger and Scallions

SERVES 6 | PREP TIME: 8 MINUTES | COOK TIME: 12 MINUTES

Nut-free • Quick & Easy   Many traditional Chinese fish dishes use the entire fish, from head to tail, but this modern recipe simplifies the process by using sea bass fillets. The sauce is full of great flavor and fragrant spice. You can also omit the chile peppers if you prefer a milder dish.

1. Season the sea bass with salt and pepper and make a couple of small diagonal cuts in the skin of each fillet.

2. Heat a wok over high heat until a drop of water sizzles on contact and add 1 tablespoon of oil.

3. In two different batches, fry the fillets, skin-side down, for 3 minutes or until the skin is crisp.

4. Turn the fillets over and cook for a further 30 seconds to 1 minute.

5. Transfer the fillets to a serving plate and cover with foil to keep warm.

6. Heat the remaining tablespoon of oil and fry the ginger, garlic, and chile peppers for 1 minute or until fragrant.

7. Remove the wok from the heat, add the scallions, and toss to combine.

8. Add the soy sauce to the wok and stir.

9. Spoon the sauce from the wok over the sea bass fillets and serve.

6 (4- or 5-ounce) sea bass fillets, with skin on

Sea salt and pepper to taste

3 tablespoons vegetable oil, divided

½ inch fresh peeled ginger, thinly sliced

2 garlic cloves, thinly sliced

2 red chile peppers, de-seeded and slivered

1 bunch scallions, thinly sliced

1 tablespoon soy sauce

6 | CHICKEN AND DUCK

Easy Sesame Chicken

SERVES 4 | PREP TIME: 15 MINUTES | COOK TIME: 10 MINUTES

Under $10 • Quick & Easy   Succulent sesame chicken is a mainstay of American-style Chinese restaurants, and the sweet soy-based sauce is full of punch and flavor. For a healthier preparation, this recipe stir-fries instead of deep-frying the chicken pieces, and the result is just as delicious as the restaurant version.

2 tablespoons soy sauce

2 teaspoons toasted sesame oil

1 tablespoon sugar

1 tablespoon honey

2 tablespoons rice vinegar

1 tablespoon grated fresh ginger

1 clove garlic, minced

1 egg, beaten

3 tablespoons cornstarch

Sea salt

Freshly ground black pepper

1 pound boneless and skinless chicken thighs, trimmed of fat and cut into bite-size pieces

1½ tablespoons peanut or vegetable oil

2 tablespoons sesame seeds, for garnish

1 scallion, sliced into ½-inch pieces, for garnish

1. In a small bowl, make the sauce by combining the soy sauce, sesame oil, sugar, honey, rice vinegar, ginger, and garlic. Set aside.

2. In a large bowl, mix the egg with the cornstarch, and season with the sea salt and pepper. Let it sit for 10 minutes. Add the chicken to the bowl with the egg mixture, and toss to coat the pieces.

3. Heat your wok on high heat until a drop of water sizzles on contact. Add the peanut oil and swirl to coat the wok. Add the chicken and stir-fry for 5 to 6 minutes, until the pieces are golden brown.

4. Add the sauce to the wok. Toss to combine it with the chicken, and continue stir-frying for about 2 minutes. As soon as the sauce thickens, turn off the heat.

5. Place the chicken on a serving platter, and garnish with the sesame seeds and scallions. Serve with rice.

Kung Pao Chicken

SERVES 4 | PREP TIME: 12 MINUTES | COOK TIME: 8 MINUTES

Under $10 • Quick & Easy   Based on a classic Sichuan dish, this version is simple to make but has tons of "pow" from the chiles. The American version is a great one to learn because you can find almost all of the ingredients at your local grocery store.

1. In a medium bowl, mix together 1 tablespoon of soy sauce, rice wine, and 2 teaspoons of cornstarch. Add the chicken, stir to coat the pieces, and let them sit for about 10 minutes.

2. In another medium bowl, mix the black vinegar, the remaining 1 teaspoon of soy sauce, the hoisin sauce, sesame oil, the remaining 1 teaspoon of cornstarch, and the ground Sichuan peppercorns. Stir to combine well and set aside.

3. Heat your wok over high heat until a drop of water sizzles on contact. Add the peanut oil and swirl to coat the wok. Add the red chiles, and stir-fry them for about 20 seconds. Then add the chicken and stir-fry until it starts to gain color, about 3 minutes. Add the scallions and garlic, and stir-fry for 1 minute.

4. Pour the sauce mixture into the wok, and toss to coat all the chicken with the sauce. Stir in the peanuts, cook for another 2 minutes, and remove the wok from the heat.

1 tablespoon plus 1 teaspoon soy sauce, divided

2 teaspoons Shaoxing rice wine or dry sherry

3 teaspoons cornstarch, divided

1 pound boneless, skinless chicken thighs, diced into small pieces

1 tablespoon Chinese black vinegar or balsamic vinegar

2 teaspoons hoisin sauce

1 teaspoon sesame oil

½ teaspoon ground Sichuan peppercorns or 1 teaspoon chili powder or chili flakes

2 tablespoons peanut or vegetable oil

8 to 10 Chinese dried whole red chiles

3 scallions, chopped

2 garlic cloves, minced

½ cup unsalted roasted peanuts

Ingredient Tip: If you can't find Chinese dried red chiles, use Mexican or Spanish dried red chiles instead. Or use 1 tablespoon of Chinese chili paste in place of the dried red chiles.

Tea-Smoked Chicken

SERVES 4 | PREP TIME: 40 MINUTES | COOK TIME: 40 MINUTES

Nut-free • *Under $10*   Smoking in general gives great flavor to chicken while keeping it moist and tender. The Chinese method of smoking with tea leaves lends a fragrant, unmistakable taste to everyday chicken. That it can be done in a simple wok in a short time will make this an often-requested meal.

¼ cup low-sodium soy sauce

5 tablespoons Shaoxing rice wine

1 tablespoon cornstarch

2 pounds skinless, boneless
   chicken thighs, trimmed of fat,
   and cut into 2-inch pieces

1 tablespoon brown sugar

¼ cup uncooked rice

¼ cup black tea leaves,
   preferably oolong

2 tablespoons
   Chinese five-spice powder

4 slices ginger

1. In a large bowl, mix the soy sauce, rice wine, and cornstarch. Add the chicken, toss to coat the pieces, and let them marinate for at least 30 minutes.

2. In a small bowl, mix together the brown sugar, rice, tea leaves, Chinese five-spice powder, and ginger. These are the ingredients used for smoking the chicken.

3. Prepare the wok to smoke the chicken. Line the bottom of your wok with a piece of aluminum foil large enough that it hangs over the edges of the wok. Place the smoking ingredients on the foil, and spread them around evenly. Place a wire rack or metal steamer basket on top of the smoking ingredients. Cover the rack with foil.

4. Place the chicken on top of the foil-covered rack, and cover it with the wok lid. Fold the overhanging foil over the wok lid. Turn the heat to medium-high. Once you start to see smoke, turn the heat down to medium.

5. Smoke the chicken for 10 minutes without removing the lid. After 10 minutes, turn off the heat. Do not remove the lid from the wok. Let the chicken smoke in the wok for another 20 minutes.

Velvet Chicken

SERVES 4 | PREP TIME: 20 MINUTES | COOK TIME: 25 MINUTES

Gluten-free • *Under $10*   Ever wonder why the chicken or meat at your local take-out place is so soft and tender? They probably "velvet" their meat before cooking it. This technique ensures super moist and soft meat, and it is simple to do: Just marinate your meat in a cornstarch mixture for 5 to 15 minutes (depending on the type of protein) before cooking it. This keeps the moisture locked in and makes sure that the meat doesn't overcook and become tough.

1. In a medium bowl, lightly beat the egg white to loosen it up, and mix it with 1 tablespoon of cornstarch. Add the chicken to the bowl, and toss to coat it with the cornstarch mixture. Let the chicken sit for at least 15 minutes.

2. In a small bowl, mix the fish sauce, lime juice, and remaining 1 teaspoon of cornstarch. Set aside.

3. Heat your wok over high heat until a drop of water sizzles on contact. Add the peanut oil and swirl to coat the wok. Add the chicken and cook for 6 to 9 minutes, tossing and stir-frying when necessary. Remove the chicken from the wok and set it aside.

4. Add more oil to the wok if necessary, and stir-fry the ginger, red bell pepper, onion, and garlic for 2 to 3 minutes. Add the fish sauce mixture to the wok, and give it a stir to combine with the vegetables. Add the chicken back to the wok, stir to combine with the vegetables, and cook for another 2 minutes.

5. Serve with chili sauce on the side. Serve with rice.

1 egg white

1 tablespoon plus 1 teaspoon cornstarch, divided

4 skinless, boneless chicken breasts, trimmed of fat and cut into bite-size pieces

1 tablespoon fish sauce

Juice of 1 lime

1 tablespoon peanut or vegetable oil, plus additional if needed

1 tablespoon grated fresh ginger

1 red bell pepper, thinly sliced

½ sweet onion, thinly sliced

1 garlic clove, thinly sliced

Chili sauce, for serving

Chicken and Sweet Corn Soup

SERVES 4 AS AN APPETIZER | PREP TIME: 5 MINUTES | COOK TIME: 15 MINUTES

Nut-free • *Under $10* • *Quick & Easy*   This soup is so nice and thick that it feels more like a gumbo or a stew. It's satisfying around the time of the first frost and equally comforting—and so quick to make—during the cold winter months. Everything you need to make this soup is at your local grocery store.

6 cups chicken broth

1 (14- to 16-ounce) can creamed corn

1 boneless, skinless chicken breast, cut into ½-inch pieces

1 tablespoon sea salt

½ teaspoon toasted sesame oil

¼ teaspoon ground white pepper

1 large egg, beaten

1. Bring the chicken broth to a boil in a wok. Reduce the heat to a low simmer, and slowly stir in the creamed corn. Add the chicken to the soup, and simmer for about 5 minutes, or until the chicken is cooked through. Add the sea salt, sesame oil, and white pepper to the soup.

2. Slowly pour the beaten egg into the soup while stirring gently. The egg will form delicate yellow strands in the soup. When it does, turn off the heat immediately, and ladle the soup into bowls to serve.

Spicy Chicken with Green Beans

SERVES 4 | PREP TIME: 10 MINUTES | COOK TIME: 10 MINUTES

Under $10 • *Quick & Easy*   This fragrant, delicious dish can be mastered at home with minimal effort. Add more chili sauce if you like it spicier, and for something special, substitute snow peas, okra, or broccolini for the green beans.

1. Parboil the green beans in a small pot for 2 to 3 minutes, until vibrant green. Drain the beans and set aside.

2. In a small bowl, mix together the soy sauce, garlic, chili sauce, and honey. Set aside.

3. Heat your wok on high heat until a drop of water sizzles on contact. Add the peanut oil and swirl to coat the wok. Add the chicken to the wok, and stir-fry for 1 to 2 minutes. Add the green beans to the wok, and continue stir-frying for about 2 minutes.

4. Pour in the soy sauce mixture and stir to combine. Continue cooking for another 2 to 3 minutes, or until the sauce has thickened slightly.

¾ **pound fresh green beans, trimmed**

2 **tablespoons soy sauce**

1 **clove garlic, minced**

1 **teaspoon chili sauce**

1 **teaspoon honey**

2 **teaspoons peanut or vegetable oil**

1 **pound boneless, skinless chicken breasts, cut into thin strips**

Chicken in Black Bean Sauce

SERVES 4 | PREP TIME: 10 MINUTES | COOK TIME: 10 MINUTES

Under $10 • *Quick & Easy*   Black bean sauce packs a powerful amount of flavor and depth, so even a small amount can transform your dish. If you have access to fermented black beans at a Chinese market, then you can make your own sauce with little effort. If not, even a prepared black bean sauce will give your dish great umami flavor. This is a simple, homey version of chicken in black bean sauce. Once you master it, you will also know how to make beef, fish, or vegetables this way.

2 tablespoons peanut oil

1 pound boneless, skinless chicken thighs, trimmed of fat and cut into bite-size pieces

1 tablespoon grated fresh ginger

2 garlic cloves, minced

1 sweet onion, thinly sliced

1 green bell pepper, cut into bite-size pieces

1 red bell pepper, cut into bite-size pieces

4 tablespoons Shaoxing rice wine or dry sherry

5 tablespoons black bean sauce

1. Heat your wok over high heat until a drop of water sizzles on contact. Add the peanut oil and then the chicken, stir-frying it for 4 to 6 minutes, or until the chicken becomes golden. Add the ginger, garlic, onion, green bell pepper, and red bell pepper, and stir-fry for another 2 minutes, or until the vegetables are crisp-tender. Add the rice wine and black bean sauce. Stir to combine.

2. Serve with rice or noodles.

Braised Duck

SERVES 4 PREP TIME | 10 MINUTES COOK TIME | 10 MINUTES

Quick & Easy   The wok can do almost anything, and that includes braising. This braised duck is simple to make and has a delicious sweet and savory sauce. If you have rice or noodles on hand, you can have dinner on the table in 15 minutes.

1. In a bowl, mix the hoisin sauce, honey, Chinese five-spice powder, and water. Set aside.

2. Heat your wok over high heat until a drop of water sizzles on contact. Add the peanut oil and swirl to coat the wok. Add the onion and stir-fry it for 2 minutes. Add the garlic and cabbage, and stir-fry for another 2 to 3 minutes. Remove the vegetables from the wok and set aside.

3. Add the duck slices to the hot wok and stir-fry for 2 minutes. Add the sauce mixture to the wok, and cook for another 2 minutes, or until the sauce thickens. Return the vegetables to the wok, and toss to combine with the duck and sauce.

4. Serve with rice or noodles.

2 tablespoons hoisin sauce

1 tablespoon honey

1 teaspoon Chinese five-spice powder

1 tablespoon warm water

1 tablespoon peanut or vegetable oil

½ small sweet onion, thinly sliced

1 clove garlic, minced

½ head napa cabbage, with leaves shredded

2 skinless duck breasts, thinly sliced

Tea-Smoked Duck

SERVES 4 | PREP TIME: 4 HOURS | COOK TIME: 25 MINUTES

Gluten-free • *Nut-free*   It's amazing how simple it is to make this beloved Sichuan recipe at home in a wok. Any trepidation you may have ever felt about cooking duck will vanish. This smoked duck has layers of flavor and is wonderful served alongside a fresh soba noodle salad or green salad.

2 tablespoons Chinese five-spice powder, plus additional, if needed

3 duck breasts, skin scored in a diamond pattern through the fat

Sea salt

Freshly ground black pepper

2 tablespoons rice wine vinegar

½ cup jasmine rice

½ cup black tea leaves, such as oolong

½ cup brown sugar

Rind of 1 lemon or 1 orange, or a combination of both

1. Rub the Chinese five-spice powder all over the duck. Season with the sea salt and pepper by sprinkling them on all sides of the duck. Place the duck breasts in a zip-top bag, and then coat them with the rice wine. Let the duck marinate for at least 4 hours in the refrigerator.

2. In a small bowl, mix the rice, tea leaves, brown sugar, and lemon rind. Set aside. These are the ingredients used for smoking the duck.

3. Prepare the smoker in your wok. Line the bottom of the wok with a piece of aluminum foil large enough that it hangs over the edges of the wok. Place the smoking ingredients on the foil, and spread them around evenly. Place a wire rack or metal steamer basket on top of the smoking ingredients. Place the duck on the rack, skin-side up, and cover the wok with a lid. Fold the overhanging foil over the top of the lid to better enclose the smoke.

4. Heat the wok on high until smoke begins to appear. Then turn the heat down to medium, and smoke the duck for 10 minutes. Do not open the wok lid. Remove the wok from the heat, and let the duck sit in the wok for 2 to 3 more minutes.

5. For crisp duck skin, place the duck breasts, skin-side down, in a hot sauté pan for 2 to 3 minutes. Remove the breasts from the pan, and let them rest for about 5 minutes.

6. Slice the duck across the grain, and serve over rice, noodles, or a salad.

General Tso's Chicken

SERVES 4 | PREP TIME: 10 MINUTES | COOK TIME: 15 MINUTES

Nut-free • Under $10 • Quick & Easy   This sweet and spicy take-out favorite is actually named after an 18th-century Chinese general. A few different restaurants claim to have invented the current version of the dish, but most agree that it was first served in New York City. You might also see it on American menus as General's Chicken or Governor's Chicken. It's usually served as a deep-fried dish, but this recipe uses wok-frying instead for crisp-tender chicken with all of the General Tso flavor.

1. In a small bowl, make the sauce by whisking together the soy sauce, rice vinegar, honey, sugar, chili sauce, chicken broth, and 2 teaspoons of cornstarch. Set aside.

2. To a medium bowl, add the remaining 3 teaspoons of cornstarch. Season with the sea salt and pepper. Add the chicken and coat it on all sides.

3. Heat your wok over high heat until a drop of water sizzles on contact. Add the peanut oil and swirl to coat the wok. Cook the chicken, making sure to get a nice brown crust on all sides. Cook it in batches, if necessary, as the chicken should not crowd the bottom of the wok. When the chicken is almost completely cooked, remove it from the wok and set it aside.

4. Turn the heat down to medium. Add the garlic, ginger, and scallions to the wok, and stir-fry for about 20 seconds. Pour the sauce into the wok, and bring it to a simmer. Return the chicken to the wok, and toss to combine with the sauce. Stir-fry the chicken for another 1 to 2 minutes, or until the chicken is cooked through.

5. Garnish the chicken with the sesame seeds and serve with rice.

3 tablespoons soy sauce

1 tablespoon rice vinegar

1½ tablespoons honey

1 tablespoon sugar

2 teaspoons chili sauce

¾ cup chicken broth

5 teaspoons cornstarch, divided

Sea salt

Freshly ground black pepper

2 pounds skinless, boneless chicken meat, cut into 1-inch pieces

2 tablespoons peanut or vegetable oil

2 garlic cloves, finely minced

2 teaspoons fresh ginger, finely minced

4 scallions, chopped

1 teaspoon roasted sesame seeds, for garnish

Hoisin Chicken

SERVES 4 | PREP TIME: 10 MINUTES | COOK TIME: 10 MINUTES

Under $10 • Quick & Easy   This tasty recipe gets lots of flavor from hoisin sauce, which includes soy sauce, chiles, garlic, sugar, and vinegar. It's similar to barbecue sauce in consistency, and you can use it in cooking sauces, as a dipping sauce, or as a condiment to flavor noodle soups.

3 tablespoons peanut or
vegetable oil, divided

1 sweet onion, sliced

1 red bell pepper, cut into strips

1 pound boneless, skinless
chicken breasts, cut into
1-inch chunks

Sea salt

Freshly ground black pepper

½ pound snow peas, washed and
trimmed

⅓ cup hoisin sauce

⅓ cup roasted peanuts

Chili sauce, for garnish (optional)

1. Heat your wok over high heat until a drop of water sizzles on contact. Add 1½ tablespoons of peanut oil, and swirl to coat the wok. Stir-fry the onion and red bell pepper for 3 to 5 minutes, until they are slightly browned. Remove the vegetables from the wok and set aside.

2. Add the remaining 1½ tablespoons of peanut oil to the wok, and stir-fry the chicken for 2 to 3 minutes, until it is browned on all sides. Season the chicken with the sea salt and pepper. Add the snow peas to the wok, and toss to combine with the chicken. Reduce the heat to medium-low and add the hoisin sauce. Cook for 1 to 2 minutes, or until the snow peas are wilted.

3. Remove the wok from the heat, sprinkle the chicken and peas with the peanuts, and serve with the chili sauce on the side (if using).

Lemon Chicken

SERVES 4 | PREP TIME: 20 MINUTES | COOK TIME: 15 MINUTES

Under $10   Soft, velveted pieces of chicken are deep-fried and deliciously paired with a sweet and tart sauce in this dish. Popular all over the world except in China, lemon chicken is a take-out favorite that isn't hard to make at home.

1. In a large bowl, mix the rice wine, soy sauce, and salt. Add the chicken to the bowl, toss it to coat on all sides, and marinate the chicken for at least 15 minutes.

2. In a small bowl, make a batter by combining the eggs, 3 tablespoons of cornstarch, and the baking powder.

3. In your wok, heat the peanut oil to 350°F. Dip each chicken breast into the batter, and then gently fry them until lightly browned, 3 to 4 minutes. When the chicken is finished, remove it with a slotted spoon, and place it on a paper towel–lined plate. Discard the oil left in the wok, and wipe the wok clean with a paper towel.

4. In a medium bowl, make the sauce by mixing the sugar, the remaining ½ tablespoon of cornstarch, the chicken broth, lemon juice, and salt.

5. Heat your wok over medium heat. Add the lemon sauce. When the sauce begins to bubble, add the lemon slices, stir, and then turn off the heat.

6. Pour the lemon sauce over the chicken and serve.

2 teaspoons Shaoxing rice wine or dry sherry

1 tablespoon soy sauce

½ teaspoon salt

2 pounds skinless, boneless chicken breast meat

2 eggs, beaten

3½ tablespoons cornstarch, divided

⅓ teaspoon baking powder

1½ cups peanut or vegetable oil

3 tablespoons sugar

⅔ cup chicken broth

1 tablespoon lemon juice

½ teaspoon salt

1 lemon, sliced into thin rounds

Spicy Chicken with Cashews

SERVES 4 TO 6 | PREP TIME: 15 MINUTES | COOK TIME: 10 MINUTES

Under $10 • Quick & Easy   One thing to admire about American-style Chinese cooking is the liberal way that fruits and nuts are thrown into the mix. Mango stir-fried with chicken? Sure! Cashews and pineapple in the fried rice? Delicious! This recipe is easy to pull off, and it has lots of heft and protein from the chicken thighs and the cashews. It does not, however, double down on sugar and oil, the way restaurants often do.

2 pounds skinless, boneless chicken thighs

Sea salt

Freshly ground black pepper

3 tablespoons peanut or vegetable oil, divided

1 cup unsalted roasted cashews

1 teaspoon crushed dried chile pepper

1 tablespoon honey

2 jalapeño peppers, deseeded and thinly sliced

1 large sweet onion, cut into large chunks

2 tablespoons oyster sauce

¼ cup chicken broth

1 scallion, chopped, for garnish (optional)

1. Cut the chicken into 1-inch pieces, and season the pieces by sprinkling them on all sides with the sea salt and pepper.

2. Heat your wok over high heat until a drop of water sizzles on contact. Add 1 tablespoon of peanut oil, and swirl to coat the wok. Add the cashews and stir-fry and toss for about 30 seconds. Transfer the nuts to a medium bowl, and toss them with the chile pepper and honey. Set aside.

3. Add the remaining 2 tablespoons of peanut oil to the wok. Add the chicken to the wok, and stir-fry for 4 to 5 minutes. Add the jalapeños and onion to the wok, and stir-fry for about 2 minutes. Add the oyster sauce, chicken broth, and cashew mix to the wok and stir to combine. Season with additional sea salt and pepper, if necessary.

4. Transfer the chicken and cashews to a platter, and garnish with the chopped scallion (if using).

Crispy Soy-Honey Chicken Wings

SERVES 3 | PREP TIME: 10 MINUTES | COOK TIME: 45 MINUTES

These saucy wings are crispy on the outside and tender on the inside like deep-fried chicken, but wok-frying them ensures that they're healthier for you. The chicken wings are baked before being quickly wok-fried, and the delectable sauce is nicely spicy and sweet.

1. Preheat the oven to 350°F.

2. Bake the chicken wings on a parchment-lined pan for 30 minutes, turning once.

3. In a large bowl, mix the cooked chicken with the minced garlic and ginger powder.

4. Heat your wok over high heat until a drop of water sizzles on contact. Add the oil and then fry the chicken in batches, adding more oil if needed.

5. Remove the chicken when the skin is crispy and brown.

6. Turn the heat under the wok down to low and then add the fish sauce, soy sauce, honey, and chili-garlic sauce.

7. Cook until the sauce starts to bubble.

8. Add the chicken back to the wok and toss to coat with the sauce.

9. Garnish with the scallion, if using.

24 chicken wingettes

3 garlic cloves, minced

1 teaspoon ginger powder

1 tablespoon peanut oil, more if needed

½ tablespoon fish sauce

2 tablespoons soy sauce

6 tablespoons honey

3 tablespoons chili-garlic sauce

1 scallion, chopped (optional)

Ingredient Tip: If you can't find wingettes, or "party wings" as they're sometimes called, use regular chicken wings. Prep the wings by cutting off the tips and halving them at the joint. A pack of 12 will get you 24 wingettes.

7 | NOODLES AND RICE

Cantonese Soy Sauce Noodles

SERVES 4 | PREP TIME: 5 MINUTES | COOK TIME: 11 MINUTES

Under $10 • *Quick & Easy* • *Vegetarian*   You need only six ingredients to make this noodle dish. It makes a great side. This is simple home cooking at its best, and you can bulk this up with eggs or chicken or other vegetables if you have them, making it a full meal in and of itself.

½ pound egg noodles, dried or fresh

2 tablespoons peanut or vegetable oil

1 cup bean sprouts, rinsed and dried

2 scallions, cut on the bias into 1-inch pieces

2½ tablespoons soy sauce

½ teaspoon sesame oil

1. If using dried noodles, parboil them for 3 minutes. Drain very well before they are added to the wok.

2. Heat your wok on high heat until a drop of water sizzles on contact. Add the peanut oil and swirl to coat the wok. Add the noodles and cook for about 4 minutes while continuously tossing and stir-frying. Add the bean sprouts, scallions, soy sauce, and sesame oil to the wok, and stir-fry for another 3 to 4 minutes, or until the noodles are browned and done.

Super Easy Vegetable Lo Mein

SERVES 4 | PREP TIME: 10 MINUTES | COOK TIME: 10 MINUTES

Under $10 • Quick & Easy • Vegetarian   Lo mein is a favorite take-out dish, and it will become one of your favorites to make at home because it's quick and you can customize it with what you have in your fridge. Go veggie-heavy and add tofu. Or use leftover rotisserie chicken. Or try something different with thinly sliced American bacon.

1. In a small bowl, make the sauce by mixing the soy sauce, sugar, sesame oil, and chili sauce (if using). Set aside.

2. Heat your wok on high heat until a drop of water sizzles on contact. Add the peanut oil and swirl to coat the wok. Add the garlic, cremini mushrooms, red bell pepper, and carrots to the wok, and stir-fry for 3 to 4 minutes, tossing often. Add the snow peas and scallions, and stir-fry for another 2 to 3 minutes.

3. Add the lo mein and the sauce mixture to the wok. Toss everything together to combine, and turn off the heat. Serve immediately.

2 tablespoons soy sauce

2 teaspoons sugar

1 teaspoon sesame oil

1 teaspoon chili sauce (optional)

1 tablespoon peanut oil

2 garlic cloves, minced

1½ cups cremini or button mushrooms, sliced

1 red bell pepper, julienned

¼ cup shredded carrots

½ cup snow peas

2 scallions, cut into 1-inch pieces

½ pound lo mein, cooked according to package directions and drained well

Ingredient Tip: If you don't have lo mein, you can make this with fettuccine, spaghetti, or even soba noodles with great results.

Shrimp *Mei Fun*

SERVES 4 | PREP TIME: 30 MINUTES | COOK TIME: 10 MINUTES

Under $10   These soft rice noodles are delicious. *Mei fun* noodles are similar to angel hair pasta. This is a great recipe to use up some leftover protein in your fridge, whether it's chicken, pork, beef, Canadian bacon, shrimp, or tofu.

1 tablespoon Shaoxing rice wine

1 teaspoon sugar

1 tablespoon soy sauce

1 tablespoon oyster sauce

1 teaspoon sesame oil

2 tablespoons peanut or
   vegetable oil

1 onion, thinly sliced

1 clove garlic, minced

1 red bell pepper,
   sliced into strips

1 cup shrimp, pork, chicken,
   beef, or tofu, thinly sliced

2 eggs, beaten

10 ounces rice noodles,
   soaked according to package
   directions, drained well

1 scallion, cut into slivers

1. In a small bowl, make the sauce by combining the rice wine, sugar, soy sauce, oyster sauce, and sesame oil. Set aside.

2. Heat your wok on high until a drop of water sizzles on contact. Add the peanut oil and swirl to coat the wok. Add the onion, garlic, and red bell pepper, and stir-fry for about 20 seconds. Add the shrimp and stir-fry for 1 to 2 minutes. Slowly stream in the eggs to create egg threads, and stir-fry for about 1 minute more. Add the rice noodles and stir-fry for about 2 minutes, tossing everything together.

3. Add the sauce mixture to the wok. Stir-fry for 1 to 2 minutes, making sure everything is combined. Add the slivered scallion, give it a quick toss, and turn off the heat.

4. Serve with rice and chili sauce or *sambal oelek* on the side.

Ingredient Tip: **Sambal oelek** *is an Indonesian chili paste. The all-purpose condiment is a flavor-packed addition to noodles, rice dishes, and soups. You can find it in the ethnic foods aisle of most supermarkets.*

Beef Chow Fun

SERVES 4 | PREP TIME: 20 MINUTES | COOK TIME: 10 MINUTES

Quick & Easy   This hits the spot when you crave a steaming hot and savory noodle dish. When paired with Spinach with Garlic (page 52) and a bottle of wine, it makes for a comforting meal with guests on a cold evening. Make it more like the traditional Cantonese classic by garnishing it with bean sprouts.

1. In a medium bowl, mix 1 tablespoon of dark soy sauce, the rice wine, and cornstarch. Add the steak to the bowl, and toss it to coat it on all sides. Let the steak marinate for about 10 minutes.

2. In a small bowl, make the sauce by combining the remaining 1 tablespoon of dark soy sauce and the light soy sauce, beef broth, and oyster sauce. Set aside.

3. Heat your wok over medium-high heat. Add the peanut oil and swirl to coat the wok. Add the onion and stir-fry it for about 1 minute. Add the steak and scallions to the wok, and stir-fry for about 1 minute, or until the beef is cooked. Add the noodles to the wok, and stir everything to combine.

4. Add the sauce mixture to the wok, and stir and toss to combine. Cook for about 2 minutes more.

2 tablespoons dark soy sauce, divided

2 teaspoons Shaoxing rice wine or dry sherry

1 teaspoon cornstarch

½ pound flank steak, cut into strips across the grain

1 tablespoon light soy sauce

⅓ cup beef or vegetable broth

1 tablespoon oyster sauce

2 tablespoons peanut or vegetable oil

1 sweet onion, thinly sliced

3 scallions, cut into 1-inch pieces

½ pound dried wide chow fun rice noodles, soaked according to package directions and drained well

Ingredient Tip: If you can't find dark soy sauce, then use 1 tablespoon teriyaki sauce and 1 tablespoon light soy sauce as a replacement.

Dan Dan Noodles

SERVES 4 | PREP TIME: 15 MINUTES | COOK TIME: 15 MINUTES

Under $10 • *Quick & Easy*   Dan dan noodles are named after the pole that street peddlers would use to carry their food. The original is a Sichuan street food of noodles in a soupy chili sauce. The American version is quite a departure from the classic recipe, but both are delicious.

2 tablespoons peanut or vegetable oil

12 ounces ground pork

Sea salt

Freshly ground black pepper

2 tablespoons fresh chopped, peeled ginger

¾ cup chicken broth

2 tablespoons chili oil

1 tablespoon rice vinegar

2 tablespoons soy sauce

½ teaspoon sesame oil

2 tablespoons peanut butter

1 teaspoon Sichuan peppercorns

½ pound dried egg noodles, cooked according to package directions, well drained

2 tablespoons chopped, roasted peanuts

3 scallions, thinly sliced

1. Heat your wok over medium heat. Add the peanut oil and swirl to coat the wok. Add the pork, season it with the sea salt and pepper, and stir-fry it for about 2 minutes. Add the ginger and stir-fry it with the pork for about 2 minutes.

2. Add the chicken broth, chili oil, rice vinegar, soy sauce, sesame oil, peanut butter, and Sichuan peppercorns. Mix everything well to combine, and simmer 6 to 8 minutes, until the sauce thickens.

3. Turn off the heat and remove the wok from the heat. Add the noodles, peanuts, and scallions to the wok, and toss everything together to combine. Serve immediately.

Chicken and Ginger Noodle Soup

SERVES 4 AS A MEAL | PREP TIME: 15 MINUTES | COOK TIME: 20 MINUTES

Nut-free   This noodle soup is a hearty meal in itself, and because it has noodles, you don't need to serve it with rice. Ginger has long been a part of traditional Chinese medicine, so serve this during cold and flu season as a delicious home remedy. Can't find rice stick noodles? Use dried egg noodles instead.

1. Heat your wok to medium-high heat, and then add the oil. Add the garlic, ginger, and shiitake mushrooms to the wok, and stir-fry for about 1 minute. Stir in the rice wine, reduce the heat to medium, and cook for 2 to 3 minutes. Add the chicken broth to the wok, and bring it to a hard simmer.

2. Add the chicken, scallions, and carrots to the soup, stir, and let it simmer for about 3 minutes. Then reduce the heat to low, and simmer for another 5 to 6 minutes. Add the soy sauce to the soup, stir to combine, and then season with the sea salt and pepper.

3. Divide the noodles among 4 soup bowls. Ladle the soup over the noodles and serve.

2 teaspoons vegetable oil

2 tablespoons minced garlic

⅓ cup finely chopped, peeled fresh ginger

5 ounces fresh shiitake or cremini mushrooms, stemmed and thinly sliced

½ cup Shaoxing rice wine or good dry sherry

6 cups low-sodium chicken broth

1½ pounds boneless chicken thighs, trimmed of fat and cut into bite-size pieces

5 scallions, green part only, cut into 1-inch pieces

3 carrots, cut into matchsticks

2 tablespoons soy sauce

Sea salt

Freshly ground black pepper

½ pound rice stick noodles, soaked in boiling water for 10 minutes and then drained

Low-Carb, Low-Cal
Shirataki Stir-Fry

SERVES 4 | PREP TIME: 12 MINUTES | COOK TIME: 15 MINUTES

Quick & Easy   *Shirataki* noodles are made out of *konjac* yams, and they are naturally low-calorie and low-carb. They might also be labeled Miracle Noodles at the store. Use them instead of a wheat noodle if you're following a low-carb, low-cal, or gluten-free diet.

1 pound *shirataki* noodles

¼ cup soy sauce

2 teaspoons hoisin sauce

1 tablespoon cornstarch

½ cup warm or room
   temperature water

1 tablespoon peanut oil

2 cups broccoli florets

½ pound boneless, skinless
   chicken breast, cut into
   thin strips

1 cup bean sprouts, washed and
   dried well

½ cup chopped cremini
   mushrooms

½ cup thinly sliced zucchini

¼ cup shredded carrots

2 scallions, chopped

1. Rinse the *shirataki* noodles very well under cool running water. After draining them well, use cooking shears to cut them into smaller pieces twice. Set aside.

2. In a small bowl, make a sauce by combining the soy sauce, hoisin sauce, cornstarch, and water. Set aside.

3. Heat your wok over medium-high heat. Add the oil and swirl to coat the wok. Add the broccoli and chicken, and stir-fry for 5 to 6 minutes, or until the chicken is cooked. Add the bean sprouts, mushrooms, zucchini, carrots, and scallions, and stir-fry for 2 to 3 minutes.

4. Pour the sauce into the wok, stir to combine it with the chicken and broccoli, and cook until the sauce has thickened, about 2 minutes. Add the noodles to the wok, mix them with the other ingredients, and cook, stirring occasionally, for 2 to 3 minutes, until the flavors are combined.

Chicken Chow Mein

SERVES 4 | PREP TIME: 15 MINUTES | COOK TIME: 15 MINUTES

Under $10 • *Quick & Easy*   Chow mein means simply "fried noodles" in Mandarin, so there is no standard ingredient list for the dish. There are countless ways to prepare stir-fried noodles, but in America, chow mein usually means fried noodles tossed in a sweet soy sauce with onions and other vegetables.

1. In a small bowl, make the sauce by combining the ginger, garlic, ketchup, oyster sauce, soy sauce, and water. Set aside.

2. Boil the noodles for 4 minutes or according to the package directions. Drain the noodles well and set aside.

3. Heat your wok over high heat until a drop of water sizzles on contact. Add the oil and swirl to coat the wok. Add the chicken and stir-fry it for about 1 minute. Add the green bell pepper and celery, and stir-fry for another 1 to 2 minutes.

4. Add the sauce to the wok. Cook and stir until the sauce starts to simmer. Add the noodles and scallions to the wok, and stir to combine the ingredients and coat the noodles with the sauce. Turn off the heat and serve.

1 teaspoon ground ginger

2 garlic cloves, minced

3 tablespoons ketchup

1 tablespoon oyster sauce

2 tablespoons soy sauce

3 tablespoons water

3 nests egg noodles

1 tablespoon peanut oil

2 small chicken breasts, cut into strips

1 large green bell pepper, cut into strips

1 celery stalk (not from the outside), cut into strips

4 scallions, trimmed and cut into 1-inch strips

Singapore Rice Noodles

SERVES 4 | PREP TIME: 20 MINUTES | COOK TIME: 15 MINUTES

Under $10   This lovely noodle stir-fry is actually from the Malaysian peninsula, but it's extremely popular in China and found on most American Chinese restaurant menus. The addition of curry or turmeric powder gives it a nice southeastern flavor.

½ cup chicken broth

¼ cup soy sauce

2 tablespoons Shaoxing rice wine

2 teaspoons minced garlic

½ teaspoon ground ginger

1 teaspoon *sambal oelek*

1 tablespoon peanut oil

2 bell peppers, 1 red and 1 green, if possible, thinly sliced

2 shallots, thinly sliced

1½ cups bean sprouts

1 teaspoon curry powder

1 cup sliced mushrooms, preferably shiitake

6 ounces thin rice noodles, soaked according to package directions, drained well

1 scallion, sliced (optional garnish)

1. In a medium bowl, make the sauce by combining the chicken broth, soy sauce, rice wine, garlic, ginger, and *sambal oelek*. Set aside.

2. Heat your wok over high heat until a drop of water sizzles on contact. Add the oil and swirl to coat the wok. Add the bell peppers, shallots, bean sprouts, and curry powder, and stir-fry for 2 to 3 minutes. Add the mushrooms and stir-fry for another 2 minutes, or until the peppers are crisp-tender.

3. Reduce the heat to medium, and add the noodles to the wok with 3 tablespoons of the sauce. Stir-fry and toss so that the noodles and sauce are combined with the other ingredients, about 2 minutes.

4. Turn off the heat and slowly pour in the remaining sauce, mixing everything to combine. Don't use all the sauce if you like it with less.

5. Serve the noodles garnished with the sliced scallion (if using).

Take-out Cold Sesame Noodles

SERVES 4 | PREP TIME: 12 MINUTES | COOK TIME: 5 MINUTES

Under $10 • Quick & Easy   These cold sesame noodles used to be popular on take-out menus, went out of style, and are now making a comeback. Food historians say this preparation started in New York and spread to the rest of the country. The sweet and spicy sauce is wonderfully satisfying and easy to make.

1. In a small bowl, mix the peanut butter, tahini paste, soy sauce, honey, black vinegar, sesame oil, and chili oil. If the peanut butter is too stiff, microwave everything for 30 seconds at 50 percent power, and stir well to combine the ingredients.

2. Heat your wok on medium-high heat. Add the peanut oil and swirl to coat the wok. Add the noodles and stir-fry for about 1 minute. Add the peanut butter sauce to the wok, and stir-fry for 1 to 2 minutes.

3. The noodles can be served at room temperature or cold. If serving cold, chill them in the refrigerator. Garnish with the scallions before serving.

2½ tablespoons creamy peanut butter

2½ tablespoons tahini paste

3 tablespoons soy sauce

1 tablespoon honey

2 teaspoons Chinese black vinegar, rice vinegar, or balsamic vinegar

1½ tablespoons sesame oil

2 tablespoons chili oil

1 tablespoon peanut oil

12 ounces fettuccine noodles or spaghetti, cooked according to package directions, drained well

3 scallions, chopped, for garnish

Ingredient Tip: A combination of peanut butter and tahini works best, but you can use only creamy peanut butter if you don't have tahini on hand. Just double the amount.

Chilly Chinese Noodles

SERVES 4 | PREP TIME: 10 MINUTES, PLUS 1 HOUR TO CHILL | COOK TIME: 5 MINUTES

Vegetarian • *Nut-free*   This dish is similar to cold sesame noodles in appearance but doesn't have a nutty flavor. These simple chilled noodles are delicious with just scallions, but you can also add other vegetables and cooked chicken or tofu for a heartier meal.

1 pound Chinese egg noodles, spaghetti, or linguine

⅓ cup plus 1 tablespoon sesame oil, divided

6 tablespoons soy sauce

2 tablespoons balsamic vinegar

4 tablespoons sugar

1 tablespoon sea salt

2 teaspoons chili oil

12 scallions, trimmed and cut into 1-inch pieces

1. Cook the noodles according to the package directions until they are al dente. Rinse quickly with cold water to cool.

2. Drain the noodles well, moving them around the colander so all the water is removed.

3. Line a wide flat plate with paper towels and spread out the noodles on it to make sure they are completely dry.

4. In an extra-large bowl, whisk together ⅓ cup sesame oil, the soy sauce, vinegar, sugar, sea salt, and chili oil. Add the scallions.

5. Heat up your wok on medium-high heat and add the remaining 1 tablespoon of sesame oil.

6. Using a slotted spoon, transfer the scallions to the wok and stir-fry for 1 to 2 minutes. Toss to avoid burning. Return the scallions to the sauce in the bowl.

7. Add the noodles to the bowl and toss with the sauce and scallions to combine.

8. Cover with plastic wrap and chill in the refrigerator for at least 1 hour.

9. Toss the noodles again with the sauce before serving.

Pineapple Fried Rice

SERVES 4 | PREP TIME: 15 MINUTES | COOK TIME: 10 MINUTES

Under $10 • *Quick & Easy*　Fried rice came about around the time that people learned to cook rice itself. But the addition of canned pineapple is a 20th-century phenomenon. If you have fresh pineapple, use it, and it will add a nice tart dimension to the dish.

1. In a small bowl, mix the soy sauce and sesame oil. Set aside.

2. Heat your wok over high heat until a drop of water sizzles on contact. Add the peanut oil and swirl to coat the wok. Add the garlic and onion, and stir-fry for about 2 minutes. Add the carrot, corn, and peas to the wok, and stir-fry until they are crisp-tender, 2 to 3 minutes.

3. Turn down the heat to medium, and stir in the rice, pineapple, ham, and scallions. Pour in the soy sauce mixture. Continue to stir-fry and cook until well combined, 2 to 3 minutes. Stir in the cashews, and season with the sea salt and pepper.

3 tablespoons soy sauce

1 tablespoon sesame oil

2 tablespoons peanut oil

2 garlic cloves, minced

1 sweet onion, diced

1 large carrot, julienned

½ cup sweet corn

½ cup peas, fresh or frozen

3 cups cooked long-grain rice
(day-old rice is best)

2 cups pineapple, drained
(fresh or canned)

½ cup ham or Canadian bacon

2 scallions, thinly sliced

¼ cup cashews,
halved lengthwise

Sea salt

Freshly ground black pepper

Ingredient Tip: You can bulk this up with shrimp or slivered pork, or you can streamline it by omitting the ham and peas. The pineapple and the cashews are essential.

Easy Egg Fried Rice

SERVES 4 | PREP TIME: 10 MINUTES | COOK TIME: 12 MINUTES

Under $10 • *Quick & Easy* • *Vegetarian*   This the perfect way to make a meal out of leftover rice and just a few eggs. Because soggy rice does not make a good fried rice dish, it's better to use leftover, day-old cooked rice rather than freshly cooked rice.

4 tablespoons peanut oil, divided

2 tablespoons minced garlic

2 tablespoons grated fresh ginger

1 small sweet onion, diced

4 cups cooked long-grain or jasmine rice (day-old rice is best)

4 large eggs, beaten

2 teaspoons sesame oil

4 teaspoons soy sauce

Sea salt

Freshly ground pepper

1. Heat your wok over medium-high heat. Add 3 tablespoons of peanut oil, and swirl to coat the wok. Add the garlic and ginger, and stir-fry for about 1 minute. Add the onion and stir-fry for about 3 minutes, or until the onion is tender.

2. Reduce the heat to medium. Add the rice to the wok, and stir everything together. Continue stir-frying for about 2 minutes.

3. Move the rice to the edges of the wok. Pour the eggs into the center of the wok, first adding the remaining 1 table-spoon of peanut oil, if necessary. Scramble the eggs, about 1 minute.

4. When the eggs are scrambled, turn the heat off. Mix the eggs into the rice. Add the sesame oil and soy sauce to the rice, and mix everything together. Season with the sea salt and pepper.

Shrimp Fried Rice

SERVES 4 | PREP TIME: 15 MINUTES | COOK TIME: 12 MINUTES

Quick & Easy   This light fried rice makes a comforting meal with some Wonton Soup (page 44) and Shredded Napa Cabbage Salad (page 137). To provide even more flavor and a great crunchy texture, garnish the rice with some unsalted roasted peanuts or cashews.

1. Heat your wok on high heat until a drop of water sizzles on contact. Add the peanut oil and swirl to coat the wok. Add the shrimp and rice wine, and stir-fry for 1 to 2 minutes, or until the shrimp just turns pink. Transfer the shrimp to a plate and set aside.

2. Add the eggs, scallions, and sesame oil to the wok, and stir-fry for about 1 minute. Add the cabbage and stir-fry for another 1 to 2 minutes.

3. Turn the heat down to medium-high and add the rice. Toss and mix everything together. Add the shrimp back to the wok, and mix everything together, stir-frying for 1 to 2 more minutes.

4. Turn off the heat and add the soy sauce, stirring to incorporate it. Season to taste with the sea salt and pepper, if necessary. Serve immediately.

2 tablespoons peanut oil

12 large shrimp, cleaned, shelled, and deveined

1 teaspoon Shaoxing rice wine

2 eggs, beaten

2 scallions, chopped

1 tablespoon sesame oil

4 leaves green cabbage, finely shredded

4 cups cooked jasmine or long-grain rice (day-old rice is best)

1 tablespoon soy sauce, plus more to taste

Sea salt

Freshly ground black pepper

Nasi Goreng
(Indonesian Fried Rice)

SERVES 4 | PREP TIME: 10 MINUTES | COOK TIME: 10 MINUTES

Quick & Easy A tasty fried rice from Indonesia, the ingredients change depending on who is making it; every cook has his or her own version. What makes *nasi goreng* different from other fried rices is the seasoning, as it's made with a lot of sauce. Its flavor comes from *kecap manis*, an Indonesian soy sauce that is thick and sweet. If you can't find it (locating it can be difficult), then substitute ½ tablespoon of soy sauce mixed with ½ tablespoon of honey.

2 tablespoons peanut or vegetable oil

3 garlic cloves, minced

2 teaspoons grated fresh ginger

1 cup of beef, chicken, or shrimp, thinly sliced (if desired)

2 tablespoons soy sauce

1 tablespoon *kecap manis*

1 teaspoon sesame oil

4 cups cooked long-grain or jasmine rice (day-old rice is best)

4 eggs, fried sunny-side up

Sambal oelek, for garnish

1. Heat your wok over high heat until a drop of water sizzles on contact. Add the peanut oil and swirl to coat the wok. Add the garlic and ginger, and stir-fry for about 20 seconds. Add the beef (if using) and stir-fry for 2 minutes.

2. Turn the heat down to medium-low, and add the soy sauce, *kecap manis*, sesame oil, and rice. Mix and stir to combine the ingredients. Stir-fry for another 2 to 3 minutes.

3. Serve in four portions, with a fried egg on top and *sambal oelek* on the side.

Easy Chicken Congee with Peanuts

SERVES 4 | PREP TIME: 10 MINUTES | COOK TIME: 70 MINUTES

Under $10   Congee is rice porridge, a Chinese comfort food that is traditionally enjoyed at breakfast. But it also makes a great anytime meal because you can try different seasonings and toppings every time you make it.

1. In your wok, bring the chicken broth and water to a boil. Add the rice, cover the wok, and reduce the heat to a gentle simmer. Let the rice simmer, stirring once in a while, for about 1 hour. The rice will have a porridge-like consistency.

2. Stir in the chicken and season with the sea salt. Let the congee simmer for about 5 more minutes.

3. Ladle it into bowls. Serve with the soy sauce, sesame oil, scallions, cilantro, peanuts, and chili oil on the side for individual garnishing (if using).

5 cups chicken broth

4 cups water

1 cup short-grain rice, rinsed well

2 cups cooked chicken, cut into small pieces

Sea salt

Soy sauce, for garnish (optional)

Toasted sesame oil, for garnish (optional)

Scallions, thinly sliced, for garnish (optional)

Cilantro, chopped, for garnish (optional)

Roasted unsalted peanuts, chopped, for garnish (optional)

Chili oil, for garnish (optional)

Ingredient Tip: If you can find crispy shallots and sambal oelek, *they will transport your congee to another taste dimension.*

8 | PORK, BEEF, AND LAMB

Better Beef with Broccoli

SERVES 4 | PREP TIME: 20 MINUTES | COOK TIME: 15 MINUTES

This steak stir-fry has a straightforward ingredient list, but the end result is better than take-out. Even if you're not familiar with the Chinese velveting technique of coating the meat in a cornstarch mixture before cooking, please don't skip it. It makes the meat tender and succulent.

3 tablespoons cornstarch

6 tablespoons water, divided

1 garlic clove, thinly sliced,
    or 1 teaspoon garlic powder

1 pound sirloin or chuck steak,
    cut into strips

⅓ cup soy sauce

1½ tablespoons brown sugar

1 teaspoon ground ginger

2 tablespoons peanut or
    vegetable oil, divided

4 cups broccoli florets

1 small sweet onion,
    cut into wedges

1. In a medium bowl, mix the cornstarch, 2 tablespoons of water, and garlic until smooth. Add the beef and toss to coat on all sides. Let it sit for 10 minutes.

2. In a medium bowl, mix the soy sauce, the remaining 4 tablespoons of water, the brown sugar, and the ginger until smooth. Set aside.

3. Heat your wok over medium-high heat. Add 1 tablespoon of peanut oil, and swirl to coat the wok. Add the beef and stir-fry for 2 minutes, or until the steak is slightly browned. Transfer the beef to a bowl and set aside.

4. Add the remaining 1 tablespoon of peanut oil to the wok, and then add the broccoli and onion. Stir-fry the vegetables for about 4 minutes, or until crisp-tender. Return the beef to the wok, and toss it with the vegetables. Add the soy sauce mixture to the wok, and stir to mix it with all the ingredients. Cover the wok and cook for 2 to 3 more minutes.

5. Serve over rice.

Mongolian Beef

SERVES 6 | PREP TIME: 15 MINUTES | COOK TIME: 10 MINUTES

Quick & Easy   Despite its name, Mongolian beef as we know it is not a Mongolian recipe. It's popular in American-style Chinese restaurants, and is usually made with flank steak cooked in a dark, sweet-savory sauce. It's a meat-heavy dish containing no vegetables.

1. In a medium bowl, mix the soy sauce, water, hoisin sauce, and dark brown sugar. Set aside.

2. In a large bowl, toss the steak with the cornstarch so it is coated on all sides. Allow it to sit for 10 minutes.

3. Heat your wok to medium-high heat. Add the oil and swirl to coat the wok. Add the ginger and garlic and stir-fry for about 20 seconds, making sure it doesn't burn. Add the steak and stir-fry for about 2 minutes. Transfer the steak to a bowl.

4. Add the soy sauce mixture to the wok. When it starts to simmer, return the steak to the wok and stir-fry it in the sauce for 1 to 2 minutes. Add the scallions, stir to combine, and then turn off the heat.

5. Serve with rice.

1 cup low-sodium soy sauce

¾ cup water

2 tablespoons hoisin sauce

⅓ cup dark brown sugar

2 pounds flank steak, cut into thick strips

¼ cup cornstarch

1½ tablespoons peanut oil

1 teaspoon minced fresh ginger

2 tablespoons minced garlic

4 scallions (green parts only), cut into 1-inch pieces

Orange Beef

SERVES 4 | PREP TIME: 15 MINUTES | COOK TIME: 10 MINUTES

Quick & Easy   This is one of those super fast, yummy recipes that doesn't require a trip to the Asian grocery. The take-out version says to deep-fry the beef before tossing with the sauce, but this healthier at-home version skips that step.

1 teaspoon sea salt

1 tablespoon plus 1 teaspoon
   cornstarch, divided

1 teaspoon minced garlic

1 teaspoon red pepper flakes

1 pound sirloin steak,
   cut into strips

1 teaspoon grated orange rind

¼ cup orange juice

2 teaspoons honey

1 teaspoon sesame oil

3 tablespoons soy sauce

1 tablespoon peanut oil

3 scallions, cut into 1-inch strips

1. In a large bowl, mix the sea salt, 1 teaspoon of the cornstarch, garlic, and crushed red pepper. Add the beef, tossing it to coat all sides. Let the beef sit for 10 minutes.

2. In a small bowl, make the sauce by combining the orange rind, orange juice, the remaining 1 tablespoon of cornstarch, honey, sesame oil, and soy sauce. Set aside.

3. Heat your wok over high heat until a drop of water sizzles on contact. Add the oil and swirl to coat the wok. Add the beef and scallions, and stir-fry for 1 to 2 minutes, or until the beef is cooked. Add the sauce to the wok, stir to combine, and cook about 2 minutes, or until the sauce thickens.

4. Serve with rice.

Pepper Steak

SERVES 4 | PREP TIME: 15 MINUTES | COOK TIME: 10 MINUTES

Quick & Easy   This is a classic American-style Chinese dish that has roots in a Fujian pork recipe. But bell peppers and yellow onions are not native to China, so our familiar take-out version is uniquely American.

1. In a large bowl, mix the soy sauce, sugar, cornstarch, and ground ginger, stirring until the sugar has dissolved.

2. Slice the steak across the grain into ¾-inch-thick slices. Add the slices to the cornstarch marinade, and coat them well on all sides. Let the beef sit for 10 minutes.

3. Heat your wok until a drop of water sizzles on contact. Add 1 tablespoon of peanut oil, and swirl to coat the wok. Add the beef and stir-fry it until it has browned, about 3 minutes. Add the remaining 1 tablespoon of peanut oil and the onion, and stir-fry about 2 minutes. If more oil is needed, add it to the wok. Add the bell peppers, zucchini, and scallions and stir-fry for another 3 minutes. Finally, add the cashews, stir everything to combine, and remove the wok from the heat.

4. Serve with rice.

¼ cup soy sauce

2 tablespoons sugar

2 tablespoons cornstarch

½ teaspoon ground ginger

1 pound sirloin steak

2 tablespoons peanut or
  vegetable oil, divided,
  plus additional, if needed

1 large sweet onion,
  cut into 1-inch squares

1 red bell pepper,
  cut into 1-inch squares

1 yellow bell pepper,
  cut into 1-inch squares

1 zucchini, halved and
  cut into rounds

3 scallions, cut into 1-inch strips

½ cup cashews

Seared Beef Rolls

SERVES 4 | PREP TIME: 35 MINUTES | COOK TIME: 10 MINUTES

This is not a traditional Asian dish at all, but a modern way to use your wok to make a fresh appetizer or colorful addition to a family-style meal. The seasoned beef pairs perfectly with the fresh, crisp veggies.

FOR THE MARINADE

1 tablespoon soy sauce

1 teaspoon sesame oil

Freshly ground black pepper

1 pound top round London broil

FOR THE FILLING

1 carrot, cut into 2-inch matchsticks

½ red bell pepper, cut into 2-inch matchsticks

½ green bell pepper, cut into 2-inch matchsticks

1 English cucumber, cut into 2-inch matchsticks

1 green apple, cut into 2-inch matchsticks

1 cup pea shoots

FOR THE SAUCE

1 tablespoon oyster sauce

2 teaspoons soy sauce

1 tablespoon Shaoxing rice wine or dry sherry

1 garlic clove, minced

4 tablespoons canned chicken or beef broth

FOR THE BEEF ROLLS

1 tablespoon peanut or vegetable oil

TO PREPARE THE MARINADE

In a large bowl, mix the soy sauce and sesame oil. Season with the pepper. Add the beef and coat it all around. Marinate the beef for at least 30 minutes.

TO PREPARE THE FILLING

In a large bowl, mix the carrot, red bell pepper, green bell pepper, cucumber, apple, and pea shoots. Set aside.

TO PREPARE THE SAUCE

In a saucepan, mix the oyster sauce, soy sauce, rice wine, garlic, and chicken broth. Bring to a simmer and turn off the heat when the sauce thickens slightly, 1 to 2 minutes. Set aside.

TO PREPARE THE BEEF ROLLS

1. Heat your wok over high heat until a drop of water sizzles on contact. Add the peanut oil and swirl to coat the wok. Add the beef and sear it for 2 minutes on each side, or until medium-rare.

2. Transfer the beef to a cutting board, and let it rest until it's cool enough to handle. Slice the beef against the grain into thin, long pieces. Lay each beef slice on a flat surface, and top each with an equal amount of the filling. Make sure the vegetables lie flat and length-wise. Roll each beef slice and secure it with toothpicks if necessary.

3. Place the beef rolls on a serving platter, and gently drizzle them with the sauce.

Stir-Fried Beef with Mangos and Pineapples

SERVES 4 | PREP TIME: 10 MINUTES, PLUS 2 HOURS TO MARINATE | COOK TIME: 10 MINUTES

Nut-free   There are some beloved American-style Chinese dishes made with canned and fresh fruit; it's a sweet and savory mix that's fun to experiment with at home. This is one of them, which you should make with fresh mangos and pineapples, if you can, for the best result. Marinate the beef overnight for a quick and simple weeknight meal.

TO PREPARE THE MARINADE

1. In a large bowl, combine the marinade ingredients together.

2. Add the beef to the marinade, toss to combine, and marinate for at least 2 hours.

TO PREPARE THE BEEF

1. Heat a wok over high heat until a drop of water sizzles on contact. Add 1 tablespoon of oil.

2. Stir-fry the beef for about 1 minute or until mostly done.

3. Remove the beef from the wok.

4. Add the remaining 1 tablespoon of oil to the wok. Stir-fry the garlic for about 15 seconds and then add the pepper, onion, and sugar. Cook for 1 to 2 minutes, tossing frequently.

5. Add the fruit and toss to combine, just until coated, and serve immediately.

FOR THE MARINADE

2 tablespoons oyster sauce

2 tablespoons soy sauce

1 teaspoon sesame oil

1 tablespoon brown sugar

2 tablespoons Chinese rice wine

1 pound beef fillet, cut into strips

FOR THE STIR-FRY

2 tablespoons vegetable or canola oil, divided

2 cloves garlic, minced

1 green pepper, cut into large dice

1 sweet onion, cut into large dice

1 teaspoon sugar

1 cup cubed mango and pineapple

Twice-Cooked Pork

SERVES 4 | PREP TIME: 10 MINUTES | COOK TIME: 1 HOUR

The recipe name, "twice cooked," refers to the fact that the pork is boiled before it's stir-fried. The end result is moist, flavorful pork that's nicely crisped at the edges.

1 pound pork belly

1 tablespoon soy sauce

1 tablespoon Shaoxing rice wine or dry sherry

1 tablespoon spicy bean paste

1 teaspoon sesame oil

2 teaspoons sugar

1 tablespoon peanut or vegetable oil

1 tablespoon black bean sauce

1 tablespoon minced fresh ginger

3 garlic scapes, cut into 1-inch pieces

1 scallion, thinly sliced

Ingredient Tip: Use additional scallions or use leeks in place of garlic scapes.

1. In a pot of enough salted water to cover the pork, boil the pork belly for about 45 minutes, skimming the fat from the top of the water as needed. Drain and allow the pork belly to cool. Slice the pork into ¼-inch-thick pieces.

2. While the pork is cooking, mix the soy sauce, rice wine, spicy bean paste, sesame oil, and sugar in a small bowl. Set aside.

3. Heat the wok over high heat until a drop of water sizzles on contact. Add the peanut oil and swirl to coat the wok. Working in two or three batches, add the pork and stir-fry it until the pieces crisp at the edges and brown on both sides. Transfer the pork to a plate lined with paper towels. Drain any excess oil from the wok, leaving just a little in the wok for the remaining stir-fry.

4. Reduce the heat to medium-high. Add the soy sauce mixture, black bean sauce, ginger, and garlic scapes to the wok, and let them heat for 2 to 3 minutes. Return the pork to the wok, and stir-fry for 1 to 2 minutes. Transfer everything to a plate, and garnish with the sliced scallion.

Super Easy Mu Shu Pork

SERVES 4 | PREP TIME: 10 MINUTES | COOK TIME: 15 MINUTES

Quick & Easy   I love the shredded veggies and the handheld appeal of mu shu dishes, but they do take a lot of prep work. This recipe takes it easy on your knives with preshredded carrots and a premade coleslaw mix. It still tastes great and it gets your mu shu on the table in less than 30 minutes.

1. Heat your wok on high heat until a drop of water sizzles on contact. Add 1 tablespoon of peanut oil and the sesame oil to the wok, and swirl to coat the wok. Add the pork and garlic, and stir-fry for 2 to 3 minutes. Transfer the pork to a plate and set aside.

2. Wipe out the wok if necessary. Heat the wok on high heat. Add the remaining 1 tablespoon of peanut oil. Then add the scallions, carrots, and coleslaw, and stir-fry for 4 to 6 minutes, or until they are crisp-tender. Add the hoisin sauce and soy sauce to the vegetables and mix to combine. Reduce the heat to medium, and return the pork to the wok. Mix everything together and stir-fry for about 2 minutes.

3. Serve the pork and vegetables with additional hoisin sauce and tortillas on the side for taco-style wrapping.

2 tablespoons peanut or vegetable oil, divided

2 teaspoons toasted sesame oil

1 pound pork tenderloin, cut into thin strips

3 garlic cloves, minced

6 scallions, thinly sliced

1 (8-ounce) bag shredded carrots

1 (10-ounce) bag premade coleslaw mix

4 tablespoons hoisin sauce, plus additional for serving

2 tablespoons soy sauce

10 flour tortillas

Stir-Fried Shredded Pork with Garlic Chives

SERVES 4 | PREP TIME: 20 MINUTES | COOK TIME: 10 MINUTES

Under $10 • *Quick & Easy*   This easy weeknight dish gets its great flavor and fragrance from garlic chives, which are equally oniony and garlicky. In an Asian grocery, they are sometimes called Chinese leeks. If you can't find garlic chives, substitute scallions or leeks.

2 tablespoons soy sauce

1 teaspoon sugar

1 teaspoon cornstarch

¾ pound pork tenderloin, cut into thin strips

4 tablespoons peanut or vegetable oil

4 garlic cloves, minced

2 bunches garlic chives, cut into 2-inch pieces

1. In a medium bowl, mix together the soy sauce, sugar, and cornstarch. Add the pork and toss to coat it on all sides. Let the pork sit for 10 to 15 minutes.

2. Heat your wok on high until a drop of water sizzles on contact. Add the peanut oil and swirl to coat the wok. Add the garlic and stir-fry for about 30 seconds. Add the pork and stir-fry until it starts to change color. Then add the garlic chives, and continue to stir-fry until the pork is completely cooked, 2 to 3 minutes.

Wok-Braised Pork Chops

SERVES 4 | PREP TIME: 15 MINUTES | COOK TIME: 30 MINUTES

This is a tasty East-West dish using ingredients likely already in your pantry. Braising pork chops in your wok gives you tender, flavorful meat.

1. Season the pork chops on both sides with the sea salt and pepper.

2. Heat your wok over medium-high heat. Add the peanut oil and swirl to coat the wok. Brown the pork chops for about 1 minute on each side. Transfer the chops to a plate.

3. Add the onion to the wok, and stir-fry until it softens and becomes translucent, 2 to 3 minutes. Add the mushrooms, potatoes, soy sauce, and vegetable broth to the wok, and give everything a stir to combine. Return the pork chops to the wok. Heat the liquid and simmer for 15 to 20 minutes, or until the potatoes are cooked through.

4. Transfer the chops and vegetables to a platter. Leave the remaining liquid in the wok. Stir the cornstarch slurry into the liquid, and allow it to thicken, 1 to 2 minutes. Pour the sauce over the pork chops and vegetables. Serve.

4 pork chops, about 1 inch thick, trimmed of fat

Sea salt

Freshly ground pepper

2 teaspoons peanut or vegetable oil

1 large sweet onion, cut into strips

4 large dried shiitake mushrooms, rehydrated and cut into strips

4 small red-skinned potatoes, scrubbed and quartered

¼ cup soy sauce

¼ cup vegetable broth

2 teaspoons cornstarch mixed with 1 tablespoon water

Braised Pork in Soy Sauce

SERVES 4 | PREP TIME: 5 MINUTES | COOK TIME: 40 MINUTES

Under $10   This dish is traditionally made with yummy pork belly, which isn't always easy to find. It's worth making a special request at your meat counter for it. Alternatively, use pork shoulder, which is less fatty, for a healthier version of the original recipe.

3 tablespoons sugar

1 tablespoon honey

4 tablespoons soy sauce

1 tablespoon peanut or vegetable oil

1-inch piece peeled ginger, smashed and coarsely chopped

1 pound pork shoulder, cut into 1-inch pieces

1 teaspoon ground cinnamon

½ cup Shaoxing rice wine

1. In a small bowl, mix the sugar, honey, and soy sauce. Set aside.

2. Heat your wok on high heat until a drop of water sizzles on contact. Add the peanut oil and swirl to coat the wok. Add the ginger and stir-fry it for about 30 seconds. Add the pork and stir-fry it for 2 to 3 minutes, browning the pieces on all sides. Add the soy sauce mixture, along with the cinnamon and rice wine. Stir everything to combine. Bring the liquid to a gentle simmer, cover the wok, and simmer for 30 minutes.

3. Serve with rice.

Black Bean Pork and Tofu

SERVES 4 | PREP TIME: 10 MINUTES | COOK TIME: 10 MINUTES

Under $10 • *Quick & Easy*   This is a take on a traditional Chinese Sichuan dish. The combination of the tofu and black bean sauce is irresistible. This version can be made using your growing pantry of Asian staples.

1. Heat your wok over high heat until a drop of water sizzles on contact. Add the peanut oil and swirl to coat the wok. Add the pork and scallions, and stir-fry until the pork is cooked, 4 to 5 minutes.

2. Add the black bean sauce and tofu to the wok, and cook for 3 to 4 minutes, stirring to mix with the pork. It's fine if some of the tofu cubes don't retain their shape. As soon as everything is mixed together and the sauce is distributed, remove the wok from the heat. Season with the sea salt and pepper.

3. Garnish with chili sauce. Serve with rice.

1 tablespoon peanut or vegetable oil

¾ pound pork tenderloin, sliced

3 scallions, chopped

⅓ cup black bean sauce

1 pound firm tofu, cut into cubes

Sea salt

Freshly ground black pepper

Chili sauce, for garnish

Eight Treasures Stir-Fry

SERVES 4 | PREP TIME: 15 MINUTES | COOK TIME: 15 MINUTES

Quick & Easy   Eight is the ultimate lucky number in China, so you just need to have eight main ingredients—meat, vegetables, and nuts—in this dish to bring in some good fortune. Mix and match to your own tastes: You can make a vegetarian version of this with different vegetables or a seafood version with shrimp and no pork.

2 tablespoons peanut or
 vegetable oil, divided

½ block firm tofu,
 cut into ½-inch cubes

1 cup diced carrots

1 cup frozen shelled edamame,
 thawed

1 cup pork tenderloin, trimmed
 of fat, diced into ½-inch cubes

3 garlic cloves, minced

1 cup roasted unsalted peanuts

1 cup diced green bell pepper

1 cup diced zucchini

2 tablespoons Shaoxing rice wine

2 tablespoons spicy bean paste

1 teaspoon sugar

2 teaspoons sesame oil

1 teaspoon chili sauce

1. Heat your wok over high heat until a drop of water sizzles on contact. Add 1 tablespoon peanut oil, and swirl to coat the wok. Add the tofu and stir-fry for about 2 minutes. Transfer the tofu to a bowl.

2. Add the remaining 1 tablespoon of peanut oil to the wok. Add the carrots, edamame, pork, and garlic, and stir-fry for 2 to 3 minutes. Add the peanuts and stir-fry for another 2 to 3 minutes. Add the bell pepper and zucchini, and toss everything together. Stir-fry for another 2 to 3 minutes, until everything is combined.

3. Add the rice wine, bean paste, sugar, sesame oil, and chili sauce, and stir-fry until the sauce has reduced and thickened, 2 to 3 minutes.

4. Serve with rice.

Mapo Tofu

SERVES 4 | PREP TIME: 7 MINUTES | COOK TIME: 12 MINUTES

Under $10 • *Quick & Easy*   This is a classic Chinese dish. Think of it as the Chinese version of chili.

2 tablespoons peanut oil

½ sweet onion, finely chopped

½ teaspoon Chinese chili paste

1 garlic clove, minced

¼ pound ground pork

½ block firm tofu, cut into cubes

2 tablespoons black bean sauce

1 teaspoon Sichuan peppercorns

1. Heat your wok over medium-high heat. Add the oil and swirl to coat the wok. Add the onion, chili paste, and garlic, and stir-fry for about 1 minute, making sure the ingredients do not burn.

2. Add the pork and stir-fry until it is almost cooked through, 2 to 3 minutes. Lower the heat to medium, and add the tofu and black bean sauce. Stir-fry for 4 to 5 minutes. It doesn't matter if some of the tofu doesn't stay in perfect cubes.

3. Remove the wok from the heat, and sprinkle the pork and tofu with the Sichuan peppercorns. Serve over rice.

Sliced Lamb with Scallions

SERVES 4 | PREP TIME: 20 MINUTES | COOK TIME: 5 MINUTES

Under $10 • *Quick & Easy*   Traditionally a Mongolian dish, this lamb preparation is also popular in northern China. For more flavor, substitute leeks or garlic scapes for the scallions.

2 tablespoons soy sauce

3 tablespoons Shaoxing rice wine

1 tablespoon cornstarch

2 teaspoons sugar

½ pound boneless lamb, cut into thin strips

3 tablespoons peanut or vegetable oil

6 to 8 scallions, cut into 1-inch pieces

1 teaspoon ground ginger

1. In a medium bowl, mix the soy sauce, rice wine, cornstarch, and sugar. Add the lamb to the bowl, and toss to coat it on all sides. Let the lamb sit for 10 minutes.

2. Heat your wok over high heat until a drop of water sizzles on contact. Add the peanut oil and swirl to coat the wok. Add the scallions and ginger, and stir-fry for about 10 seconds, making sure the ingredients do not burn. Add the lamb and stir-fry for about 1 minute, or until completely cooked through. Serve immediately.

Hunan Lamb

SERVES 4 | PREP TIME: 35 MINUTES | COOK TIME: 5 MINUTES

This spicy lamb dish works best if you use leg of lamb. The best thing about this recipe is the combination of fragrant and spicy leeks, garlic, ginger, and chiles.

1. In a medium bowl, mix the soy sauce, sesame oil, rice wine, and sugar. Add the lamb, toss it to coat on all sides, and allow it to marinate for 30 minutes.

2. Heat your wok over high heat until a drop of water sizzles on contact. Add the peanut oil and swirl to coat the wok. Add the ginger and leeks, and stir-fry for about 1 minute. Add the chiles and garlic, and stir-fry for 1 minute.

3. Add the lamb and stir to combine it with the other ingredients. Add the hoisin sauce and cornstarch slurry to the wok, and stir until the sauce thickens, 2 to 3 minutes. If the sauce becomes too thick, add a little more water.

4. Remove the wok from the heat and serve.

2 tablespoons soy sauce

1 teaspoon sesame oil

2 teaspoons Shaoxing rice wine

1 teaspoon sugar

½ pound lamb, thinly sliced

1 tablespoon peanut or
   vegetable oil

2 teaspoons minced ginger

2 leeks, cut into 1-inch strips

3 dried chiles, Chinese red,
   Mexican, or Spanish

1 teaspoon minced garlic

2 teaspoons hoisin sauce

2 teaspoons cornstarch mixed
   with 4 tablespoons water

9 | THE BASICS

Basic Steamed White Rice

SERVES 4
PREP TIME: 2 MINUTES
COOK TIME: 30 MINUTES

Gluten-free • Nut-free • Vegan

Even though short-, medium-, and long-grain rice are all eaten in China, Chinese restaurants in America usually serve medium-, long-grain, or jasmine rice. If you don't have a rice cooker, here's the basic way to make white rice on the stove.

2 cups rice
3 cups water

1. Rinse the rice in water until the water runs clear. Drain it and place it in a heavy-bottomed pot. Add the water.

2. Bring the water to a boil, uncovered. When it is boiling, stir the rice once, reduce the heat to a low simmer, and cover the pot with a lid.

3. Cook the rice for about 15 minutes, and then remove the covered pot from the heat. Do not uncover the pot. Let the rice rest in the covered pot for another 15 minutes to continue steaming.

4. Take off the lid, fluff the rice, and serve.

Chili Oil

MAKES 1½ CUPS
PREP TIME: 5 MINUTES
COOK TIME: 3 HOURS

Gluten-free • Vegan

You can find chili oil in most large chain grocery stores and in every Asian market. But if you want to make your own to customize the level of spice, it's easy to do at home.

1 cup peanut oil
¼ cup sesame oil
½ cup crushed Chinese dried red chiles

1. In a small, heavy-bottomed saucepan, heat the peanut and sesame oils to about 250°F. Stir in the crushed red chiles. Turn off the heat immediately, and let the chiles steep in the oil for about 3 hours.

2. Strain the oil into a clean glass bottle. Store in the pantry or another cool, dark place.

Ingredient Tip: If you cannot find Chinese dried red chiles, use Mexican dried red chiles instead.

Spicy Chili Dip

MAKES ¼ CUP
PREP TIME: 5 MINUTES

Nut-free • Quick & Easy • Vegan

This is a quick dipping sauce for dumplings, fried wontons, or egg rolls.

4 tablespoons soy sauce
1 to 2 teaspoons Chinese chili sauce
½ teaspoon sesame oil

Whisk the ingredients together in a small bowl.

Dumpling Wrappers

MAKES ABOUT 50 WRAPPERS
PREP TIME: 20 MINUTES

Nut-free • Quick & Easy • Vegan

You can buy dumpling wrappers almost anywhere, but homemade ones always hold up a lot better in cooking. Use these to make any type of dumpling. Unlike store-bought wrappers, you probably won't need water to seal the edges closed.

3 cups all-purpose flour
1½ cups room temperature water
½ teaspoon salt

1. In a large bowl, mix the flour, water, and salt. Transfer the dough to a work surface, lightly floured if necessary, and knead the dough until it becomes smooth.

2. Roll the dough into a cylinder, and cut it into about 30 pieces. Roll a dough piece into a small ball. Squash it down with your palm, and then use a rolling pin to roll it into a circular wrapper, about 3 inches in diameter.

3. The wrappers can be made in advance and frozen for up to three weeks. Lay the rolled-out wrappers, with pieces of parchment paper between them, in an airtight container.

Sesame Dipping Sauce

MAKES ½ CUP
PREP TIME: 5 MINUTES

Nut-free • *Quick & Easy* • *Vegetarian*

This savory sesame dipping sauce is great with any type of dumpling or scallion pancakes.

4 tablespoons soy sauce
3 tablespoons rice wine vinegar
1 clove garlic, minced
1 tablespoon honey
1 teaspoon sesame oil
1 teaspoon sesame seeds

Whisk all the ingredients together in a small bowl.

Soy and Vinegar Dipping Sauce

MAKES ⅓ CUP
PREP TIME: 3 MINUTES

Nut-free • *Quick & Easy* • *Vegan*

Another favorite dipping sauce for dumplings or scallion pancakes, this soy and vinegar sauce always hits the spot.

3 tablespoons soy sauce
2 tablespoons Chinese black vinegar
1 teaspoon sesame oil

Whisk all the ingredients together in a small bowl.

Easy Ginger Chicken Broth

MAKES 2 QUARTS
PREP TIME: 5 MINUTES
COOK TIME: 20 MINUTES

Nut-free • Quick & Easy

When making Chinese soups and noodle bowls, it helps to have an aromatic broth on hand. With just four ingredients, you can create a fragrant soup broth.

1 quart good-quality low-sodium chicken broth

1 cup water

1-inch piece of ginger, peeled and cut into thin pieces

3 cups Shaoxing rice wine

In a large pot, bring the broth, water, ginger, and rice wine to a boil. Reduce the heat and simmer gently for about 20 minutes. Remove the ginger slices.

Kung Pao Sauce

MAKES 1¼ CUPS
PREP TIME: 5 MINUTES

Nut-free • Quick & Easy

If you make this sauce and keep it in your fridge, making Kung Pao Chicken (or kung pao pork or beef) will be a snap.

¾ cup low-sodium chicken broth

3 tablespoons soy sauce

2½ tablespoons Shaoxing rice wine

1½ tablespoons Chinese black vinegar

1 teaspoon toasted sesame oil

2 teaspoons cornstarch

Whisk the ingredients together in a small bowl. Use immediately or store in a glass jar in your refrigerator.

Ingredient Tip: If you don't have black vinegar, combine 1 tablespoon Worcestershire sauce with 1 teaspoon balsamic vinegar.

Sweet and Sour White Radish

SERVES 4 AS A SIDE
PREP TIME: 40 MINUTES

Nut-free • Vegan

You may recognize this crunchy side dish, as it's served before or alongside many dishes in Chinese restaurants. This cool and crispy "quick pickle" goes well with saucy and smoky stir-fries.

½ large daikon radish, washed and peeled
White vinegar, enough to cover the radish
6 tablespoons sugar

1. Cut the radish into thin, long strips. Place the strips in a large bowl, and cover them with the vinegar. Add the sugar and mix everything together to combine and dissolve the sugar. If necessary, use a heavy plate to keep the radish strips submerged. Let the radish sit for at least 20 minutes.

2. Serve immediately or store in your refrigerator.

Pickled Cabbage

SERVES 4 AS A SIDE
PREP TIME: 45 MINUTES

Nut-free • Vegan

Just like the Sweet and Sour White Radish, this crunchy pickled cabbage is the perfect complement to savory Chinese meals.

1 small red cabbage, cored,
    outer leaves discarded
4 to 6 Chinese dried red chiles
½ cup white vinegar
¼ cup sugar
Sprinkle of sea salt

1. Bring a pot of water to a boil. There should be enough water for the cabbage to be fully submerged. Add the cabbage and parboil it for about 10 seconds. Drain the cabbage and let it cool until it can be handled.

2. Chop the dried chiles into small pieces, and discard any seeds. In a large bowl, combine the chiles, white vinegar, sugar, and sea salt. Stir until the sugar dissolves.

3. Chop the cabbage and add it to the bowl. Mix well. Let the cabbage sit for about 30 minutes. Serve immediately or store in a glass jar in the refrigerator.

Shredded Napa Cabbage Salad

SERVES 4 AS A SIDE
PREP TIME: 20 MINUTES

Nut-free • Quick & Easy • Vegan

This crisp, bright cabbage salad is an easy and complementary side dish to your wok-prepared meals.

1 tablespoon toasted sesame oil

1 tablespoon soy sauce

3 tablespoons rice vinegar or white vinegar

1 tablespoon sugar

3 cups finely shredded napa cabbage

1 cup shredded carrots

1 scallion, finely slivered

In a large bowl, whisk together the sesame oil, soy sauce, rice vinegar, and sugar. Add the cabbage, carrots, and slivered scallion. Toss to combine.

Sriracha

MAKES 1 CUP
PREP TIME: 10 MINUTES
COOK TIME: 10 MINUTES

Gluten-Free • Nut-Free
Quick & Easy • Vegan

Sure you can buy sriracha at the grocery store, but why not make your own? That way, you can precisely control what is in it. Sriracha adds wonderful heat to foods, and it has become a very popular condiment. This recipe uses healthy, delicious ingredients.

1½ pounds spicy red chile peppers, such as red jalapeño (hotter peppers make hotter sriracha)

½ cup apple cider vinegar

10 garlic cloves, finely minced

¼ cup tomato paste

1 tablespoon tamari or coconut aminos

½ teaspoon stevia

1 teaspoon sea salt

1. Stem, seed, and chop the chile peppers.

2. In a food processor or blender, combine all of the ingredients and purée until smooth.

3. In a small saucepan, bring the purée to a simmer over medium-high heat, and cook, stirring frequently, for about 10 minutes, until it's thick.

4. Store in a sterile container in the refrigerator for up to 1 month.

GLOSSARY

Black bean sauce: This prepared sauce can be found in many grocery stores, not just Asian markets. It's a highly flavored sauce made of fermented black beans, soy sauce, sugar, and other ingredients.

Black vinegar: If a recipe calls for black vinegar, then it means Chinkiang black vinegar, which is deep and rich. Use balsamic vinegar as a substitute.

Bok choy: This delicately flavored vegetable is actually a member of the cabbage family. It can be found in Asian grocery stores and most large supermarkets. It's usually sold in bunches. Purchase only those with unblemished leaves.

Chili oil: A fiery red oil that has been infused with chile pepper, this inexpensive oil is used in dipping sauces and as an ingredient in cooked dishes.

Chili sauce: A staple in the Chinese kitchen, this red paste has bits of real chile pepper and is flavored with garlic. If unavailable, use *sambal oelek* or another prepared chili-garlic sauce.

Fish sauce: A staple in South Asian cooking, fish sauce is also used throughout East Asia to add a deep umami flavor to dishes. It may be called *nam pla* on the bottle.

Peanut oil: Peanut oil is included in most recipes because it has a high smoke point and is good for wok cooking. Use soybean oil, mild vegetable oil, or canola oil as an alternative.

Rice vinegar: Popular in Asian cooking, it is milder than other white vinegars. Use cider vinegar as an alternative.

Rice wine: If a recipe calls for rice wine, then Shaoxing (Shao-hsing) wine is best, as it's good enough to drink. If it's not available, another Asian rice wine or a dry sherry is a good substitute.

Sea salt: The varieties of sea salts tend to be coarser than table salt. If sea salt is unavailable, substitute kosher salt. To use regular table salt, use half the amount of sea salt indicated in the recipe.

Sesame oil: A richly fragrant oil made from roasted sesame seeds, Asian sesame oil adds a nutty aroma to dishes and is darker and very different from refined sesame oils. A little goes a long way, so use sparingly.

Tea leaves: For tea-smoking food, use black tea. Chinese black tea is best, especially Lapsang Souchong, but you can also use another black tea, such as oolong. Green tea is not recommended for the dishes in this book.

REFERENCES

Chiang, Cecilia. *The Seventh Daughter: My Culinary Journey from Beijing to San Francisco.* Berkeley, CA: Ten Speed Press, 2007.

Coe, Andrew. *Chop Suey: A Cultural History of Chinese Food in the United States.* New York: Oxford University Press, 2009.

Essman, Elliot. "Chinese Cuisine in the United States." *Life in the USA.* Accessed March 21, 2015. lifeintheusa.com/food/chinese.htm.

Huang, Ching-He. *Ching's Everyday Easy Chinese.* New York: William Morrow Cookbooks, 2011.

Kuan, Diana. *Chinese Takeout Cookbook.* New York: Ballantine Books, 2012.

Lin-Liu, Jen. *Serve the People: A Stir-Fried Journey Through China.* Orlando: Harcourt, 2008.

Lo, Eileen Yin-Fei. *The Chinese Kitchen: Recipes, Techniques and Ingredients, History, and Memories from America's Leading Authority on Chinese Cooking.* New York: William Morrow, 1999.

Low, Jennie. *Chopsticks, Cleaver, and Wok: Homestyle Chinese Cooking.* San Francisco: Chronicle, 1987.

Organisation for Economic Co-operation and Development, "Obesity Update" (June 2014). www.oecd.org/els/health-systems/Obesity-Update-2014.pdf.

Yan, Martin. *Martin Yan's Chinatown Cooking: 200 Traditional Recipes from 11 Chinatowns Around the World.* New York: William Morrow, 2002.

Young, Grace. *Stir-Frying to the Sky's Edge.* New York: Simon & Schuster, 2010.

Young, Grace, and Alan Richardson. *The Breath of a Wok: Unlocking the Spirit of Chinese Wok Cooking Through Recipes and Lore.* New York: Simon & Schuster, 2004.

Zeratsky, Katherine. "What Is MSG? Is It Bad for You?" The Mayo Clinic. Last modified March 13, 2015. www.mayoclinic.org/healthy-living/nutrition-and-healthy-eating/expert-answers/monosodium-glutamate/faq-20058196.

RESOURCES

Amazon, www.amazon.com, for cooking tools, Asian ingredients, and sauces.

Penzey's Spices, www.penzeys.com, for hard-to-find spices.

The Wok Shop, www.wokshop.com, for woks, cooking tools, and wok information.

Recommended Brands for Prepared Sauces and Pastes

Kikkoman

Koon Chun

Lee Kum Kee

Mae Ploy

Marukan

Pearl River Bridge

MEASUREMENT CONVERSIONS

Volume Equivalents (Liquid)

US STANDARD	US STANDARD (OUNCES)	METRIC (APPROXIMATE)
2 tablespoons	1 fl. oz.	30 mL
¼ cup	2 fl. oz.	60 mL
½ cup	4 fl. oz.	120 mL
1 cup	8 fl. oz.	240 mL
1½ cups	12 fl. oz.	355 mL
2 cups or 1 pint	16 fl. oz.	475 mL
4 cups or 1 quart	32 fl. oz.	1 L
1 gallon	128 fl. oz.	4 L

Volume Equivalents (Dry)

US STANDARD	METRIC (APPROXIMATE)
⅛ teaspoon	0.5 mL
¼ teaspoon	1 mL
½ teaspoon	2 mL
¾ teaspoon	4 mL
1 teaspoon	5 mL
1 tablespoon	15 mL
¼ cup	59 mL
⅓ cup	79 mL
½ cup	118 mL
⅔ cup	156 mL
¾ cup	177 mL
1 cup	235 mL
2 cups or 1 pint	475 mL
3 cups	700 mL
4 cups or 1 quart	1 L
½ gallon	2 L
1 gallon	4 L

Oven Temperatures

FAHRENHEIT (F)	CELSIUS (C) (APPROXIMATE)
250°	120°
300°	150°
325°	165°
350°	180°
375°	190°
400°	200°
425°	220°
450°	230°

Weight Equivalents

US STANDARD	METRIC (APPROXIMATE)
½ ounce	15 g
1 ounce	30 g
2 ounces	60 g
4 ounces	115 g
8 ounces	225 g
12 ounces	340 g
16 ounces or 1 pound	455 g

RECIPE INDEX

INDEX